跟我学汉语

学生用书　第一册

Learn Chinese with Me

Student's Book 1

Printed in China

人民教育出版社

People's Education Press

跟我学汉语

学生用书　第一册

（英语版）

*

人民教育出版社出版发行

网址：http://www.pep.com.cn

人民教育出版社印刷厂印装　全国新华书店经销

*

开本：890 毫米×1 240 毫米　1/16　印张：15.5

2003 年 3 月第 1 版　2009 年 12 月第 11 次印刷

印数：73 501～83 500 册

ISBN 978-7-107-16422-4 / G·9512（课）　定价：60.00 元（附 2 张 CD）

教材项目规划小组

严美华　姜明宝　张少春

岑建君　崔邦焱　宋秋玲

赵国成　宋永波　郭　鹏

主　　编　陈　绂　朱志平

编写人员　朱志平　徐彩华　娄　毅

宋志明　陈　绂

英文翻译　李长英

责任编辑　施　歌

审　　稿　王本华　吕　达

美术编辑　张立衍

插图制作　北京天辰文化艺术传播有限公司

前　言

《跟我学汉语》是一套专为海外中学生编写的汉语教材，使用对象主要是以英语为母语的中学生或者年龄在15岁～18岁的青少年第二语言学习者。

《跟我学汉语》凝聚了我们这些从事并热爱汉语教学的教师们的大量心血。这套教材从框架的设计到语言材料的选取安排，都吸收了当前汉语作为第二语言习得研究、特别是对以英语为母语的汉语习得研究的最新成果。由于编写者都是汉语作为第二语言教学的教师，因此能够从自己亲身进行教学的角度去设计教材，安排内容。在编写的过程中，我们也多次征求并采纳了海外中学以汉语为第二语言进行教学的一线教师的意见，这些意见给予了编写工作很好的启示。

《跟我学汉语》这套教材以零为起点，终点接近中级汉语水平。编写的主导思想是培养海外中学生学习汉语的兴趣。教材在内容的安排上力图自然、有趣，符合第二语言学习规律。教材语法点的出现顺序以表达功能的需要为基础，并用话题为线索来编排语言材料，从而带动交际能力的培养。《跟我学汉语》采用的话题得益于海外广大中学生的热情贡献。2001年编者在北美地区对两个城市的中学生进行了“你感兴趣的话题”的问卷调查，这套教材的话题即是从500多份调查材料中精心筛选出来的。我们希望，这套教材能够在不失系统性的基础上，表现出明显的功能性；在不失科学性的基础上，表现出明显的实用性；在不失严肃性的基础上，表现出明显的趣味性。

《跟我学汉语》全套教材共12册，包括学生用书4册以及配套的教师用书、练习册各4册，同时有与学生用书相配套的语音听力材料和多媒体教材。全套教材可供英语地区中学汉语教学9年级～12年级使用。

《跟我学汉语》是中国国家对外汉语教学领导小组办公室（简称国家汉办）所主持的一项重点研究项目的一部分，由北京师范大学承担。在编写这套教材的过程中，我们得到了方方面面的支持与帮助。为此，我们衷心感谢：

国家汉办严美华主任、姜明宝副主任、李桂苓女士、宋永波先生,他们的具体指导给予了教材编写最为有力的帮助;

加拿大温哥华、多伦多地区的汉语教师：Jean Heath, Kate McMeiken, Tina Du, Chong Fu Tan, Hua Tang, Larry Zehong Lei, Assunta Tan A.M.,Maggie Ip,Billie Ng, Yanfeng Qu, Hilary Spicer, Tina Ding, Xue Wu，王献恩，李建一，高锡铭，戴大器，宋乃王……他们在教材的前期调研中提供了大量的帮助，在他们的帮助下，我们走近了北美地区，走近了我们要编写的教材；

美国芝加哥地区的汉语教师：纪瑾、车幼鸣、谢洪伟、李迪、傅海燕、顾利程，他们认真地试用了教材的初稿，并提出了宝贵的意见；

中国驻加拿大温哥华总领事馆教育参赞许琳女士、中国驻加拿大多伦多总领事馆教育参赞张国庆先生，他们以及他们的同事为教材的前期调研提供了大量帮助，为教材的编写付出了许多心血和精力，他们的热情和坦诚都令人感动；

中国驻美国芝加哥总领事馆教育组的江波、朱宏清等先生，他们为这套教材的试用与修改做了许多工作；

国家汉办原常务副主任、北京语言学院副院长程棠先生认真地审阅了全部学生用书、教师用书和练习册，并提出了中肯的意见。

在教材编写的初期和后期，国家汉办先后两次组织专家对教材的样课和定稿进行了审定，专家们提出了许多宝贵意见，我们在此一并致谢。

编　者

2003年6月

Preface

Learn Chinese with Me is a series of textbooks designed especially for overseas high school students. It is mainly targeted at students of Chinese language, aged between 15 and 18 years old, whose native language is English.

Learn Chinese with Me is a product of many years' painstaking labor carried out with a passion and devotion to the cause of Chinese teaching. During the process of compiling this series (from the framework design to the selection and arrangement of the language materials), we have taken into consideration the latest research on the acquisition of Chinese as a second language, especially on the acquisition of Chinese by English-speakers, our own experiences of teaching Chinese as a second language and feedback from numerous other Chinese language teachers working on the front line. We were able to design the textbooks and arrange the content on the basis of a wide spectrum of knowledge and experience, both academic and practical.

This series of textbooks guides the students from beginner to low-intermediate level. The compiling principle is to foster high school students' interest in learning Chinese. The content is natural and interesting and arranged in accordance with the rules of learning a second language. To cope with the general needs of conducting daily communication, the sentence patterns and grammar are presented to students in an order that emphasizes functional usage and the language materials are arranged within situational topics. The selection of these topics owes a great deal to overseas high school students themselves. In 2001, we conducted a survey among high school students in two North American cities on *Topics That You're Interested in*, and the topics in this series of textbooks have been carefully selected based on this survey of over 500 questionnaires. It is our goal that this textbook series is, on the one hand, functional, pragmatic and interesting to the learner, and on the other hand, systematic, scientific, and academic.

The entire series of *Learn Chinese with Me* is composed of 12 books, including 4 Student's Books, 4 Teacher's Books, 4 Workbooks and other phonetic and listening materials and multimedia materials supplemented to the Student's Books. The series can meet the needs of teaching Chinese to 9-12 grades in English-speaking countries and communities.

This series of textbooks is part of a major project sponsored by China National Office for Teaching Chinese as a Foreign Language (NOCFL) and entrusted to Beijing Normal University to carry out. During the whole compiling process, we received assistance and support from various parties. Therefore, we'd like to dedicate our gratitude to:

Yan Meihua, Director of NOCFL, Jiang Mingbao, Vice Director of NOCFL, Ms. Li Guiling and Mr. Song Yongbo. Their specific directions have been of crucial assistance to us.

We would also like to thank the teachers in Vancouver and Toronto, Canada. They are Jean Heath, Kate McMeiken, Tina Du, Chong Fu Tan, Hua Tang, Larry Zehong Lei, Assunta Tan A.M., Maggie Ip, Billie Ng, Yanfeng Qu, Hilary Spicer, Tina Ding, Xue Wu, Xian'en Wang, Jianyi Lee, Ximing Gao, Daqi Dai and Naiwang Song etc. Through their help in the area of research and their valuable suggestions, we acquired a better knowledge of the North American classroom and finally came closer than ever before to the kind of textbook we have always strived to create.

The teachers of Chinese in Chicago, Jin Ji, Youming Che, Hongwei Xie, Di Lee, Haiyan Fu and Licheng Gu also provided valuable suggestions after they carefully read the first draft of the textbook.

We also really appreciate the great assistance offered by Ms. Xu Lin, Educational Attaché of the General Chinese Consulate in Vancouver, Canada and Mr. Zhang Guoqing, Educational Attaché of the General Chinese Consulate in Toronto, Canada. They and their colleagues gave us lots of help during our long-time survey for this book. Their devotion, enthusiasm and sincerity for the project has deeply impressed us.

Mr. Jiang Bo and Mr. Zhu Hongqing in charge of education in General Chinese Consulate in Chicago also made many contributions to the trial use and revision of this series.

In addition, we would like to give our special thanks to Mr. Cheng Tang, the former Vice Director of the Standing Committee of NOCFL and the Vice President of Beijing Language Institute. He made many critical proposals to us based on his careful study of all the Student's Books, the Teacher's Books and the Workbooks, and offered some invaluable suggestions.

At both the beginning and late stages of compiling this textbook series, NOCFL twice organized experts to examine and evaluate the textbook sample and the final draft. These experts, too, provided useful comments on the series. We are also grateful to them.

Compilers

June, 2003

Where is China?

长城(Chángchéng)
The Great Wall

天坛(Tiāntán)
The Temple of Heaven

黄山(Huángshān)
The Yellow Mountains

兵马俑(bīngmǎyǒng)
Terracotta warriors and horses

What do you know about China?

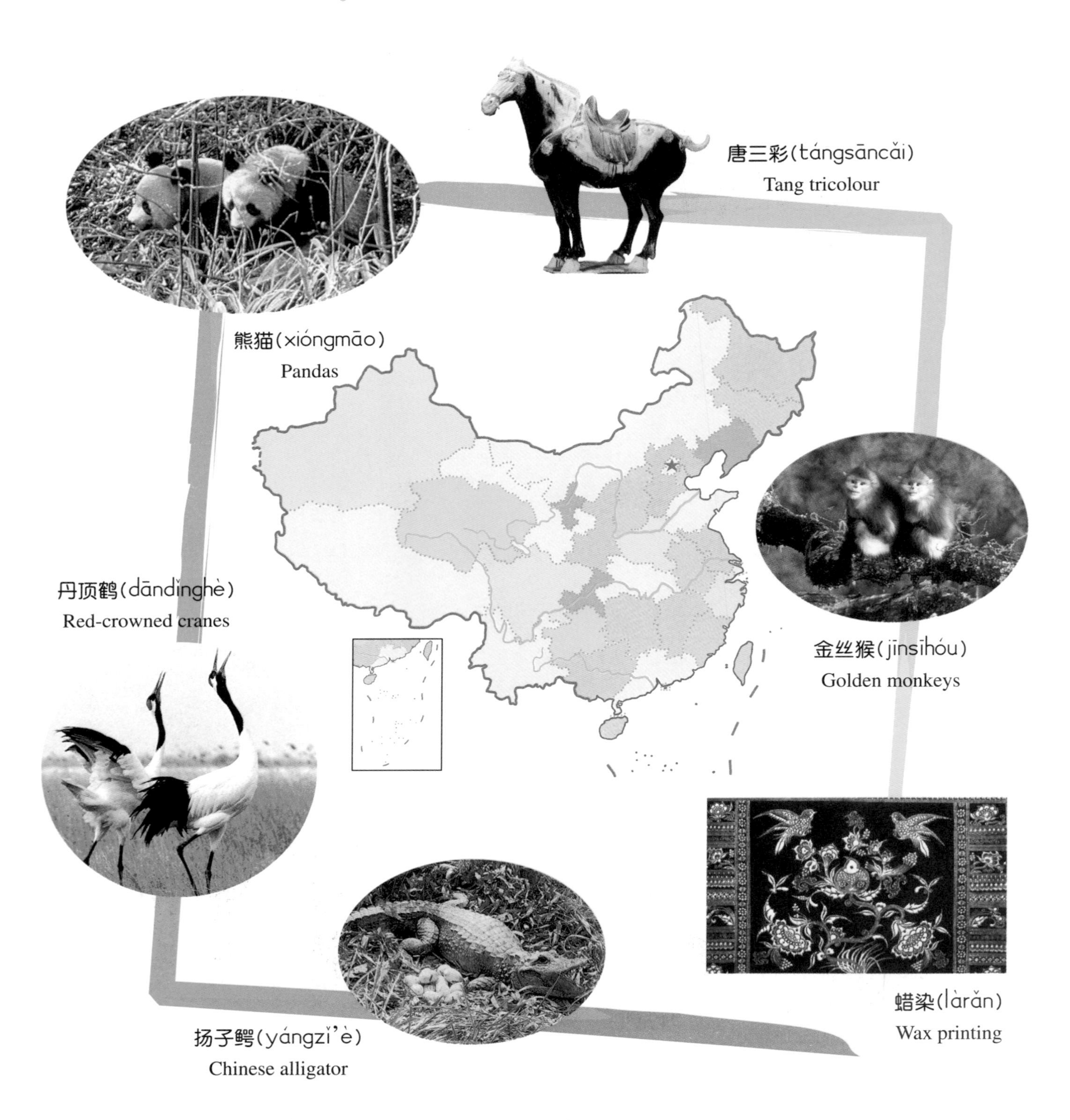

Enjoy the Chinese Knot and Try to Make One

The Chinese knot is one of China's unique folk arts. This traditional hand made folk art is made of rope or string. It has many distinctive shapes and splendid colors. Each basic type is given a name according to its shape and meaning. Chinese knots are rich in cultural symbolism. For example, the ten thousand blessing knot is also called the knot of dreams coming true and symbolizes good fortune and best wishes.

万字结(wànzìjié)
Ten thousand blessing knot

双喜结(shuāngxǐjié)
Double happiness knot

草花结(cǎohuājié)
Straw flower knot

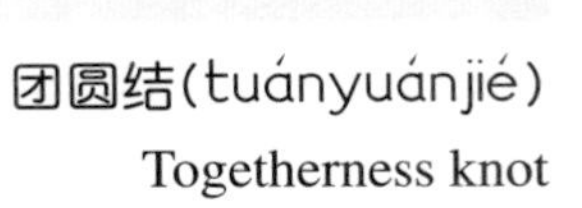

团圆结(tuányuánjié)
Togetherness knot

CONTENTS

Chinese Phonetic Transcription (*Pinyin*)

1. Formula for the Chinese Phonetic Transcription (*Pinyin*).

initials	b p m f	d t n l
	g k h	j q x
	zh ch sh r	z c s

finals	simple finals	a	o	e	i	u	ü
	compound finals	ai ao	ou	ei	ia ie iao iou	ua uo uai uei	üe
	nasal compound finals	an ang	ong	en eng	ian in iang ing iong	uan uen uang ueng	üan ün

2. Tones.

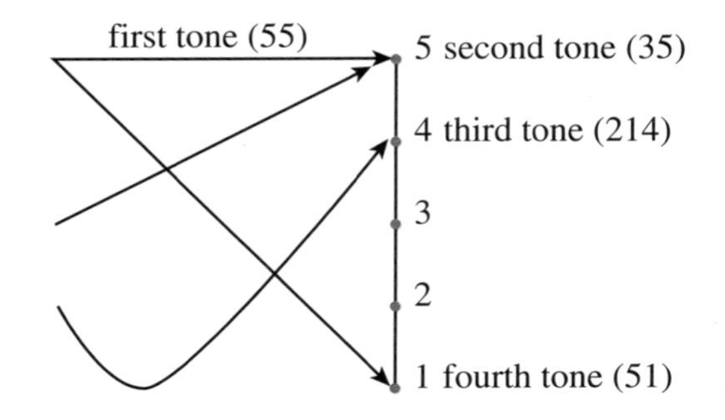

3. A Chinese syllable is made up of initials, finals and a tone. For example:

initials	finals	tones	syllables
n	i	ˇ	nǐ
h	ao	ˇ	hǎo

4. A difference in tone means a difference in meaning.

mā (mum) má (flax) mǎ (horse) mà (to swear)

wēn (lukewarm) wén (to smell) wěn (to kiss) wèn (to ask)

fāng (square) fáng (house) fǎng (to visit) fàng (put down)

qī (seven) qí (to ride) qǐ (get up) qì (angry)

Unit One

School, Classmates and Teachers

Look and Say

1 你好
nǐ hǎo

Wang Jiaming, a freshman, is meeting his classmate for the first time.

家明：你好！	Jiāmíng: Nǐ hǎo.
大卫：你好！	Dàwèi: Nǐ hǎo.
家明：我叫王家明。	Jiāmíng: Wǒ jiào Wáng Jiāmíng.
大卫：我叫大卫。	Dàwèi: Wǒ jiào Dàwèi.

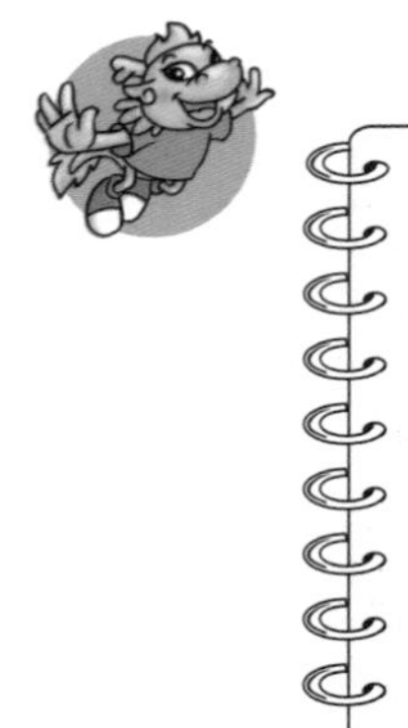

New words

1. 你 nǐ (pron.) you
2. 好 hǎo (adj.) good
3. 我 wǒ (pron.) I; me
4. 叫 jiào (v.) call; name

Proper nouns

- 王家明 Wáng Jiāmíng Wang Jiaming
- 大 卫 Dàwèi David

Read, then practice with a partner.

On your own: Complete the following dialogues.

A: Nǐ hǎo, wǒ _____ Emma Williams.

B: __________ , __________ Alice Harris.

A: Zǎoshang hǎo, Bob.

B: __________ , Charlie.

Class activity

Do you have a Chinese name? If you don't, choose one for yourself. If you do, write it on the blackboard and tell us what does it mean.

common boy's names

家 family jiā　伟 great wěi　军 army jūn

明 bright míng　光 light guāng　凯 victorious kǎi

common girl's names

美 beautiful měi　芳 fragrant fāng　淑 fair, kind and gentle shū

云 cloud yún　梅 plum méi　娟 graceful juān

① Good morning.

② Good evening.

Phonetics

1. Read the following sounds.

initials	finals	tones	syllables	
	uo	ˇ	wǒ	
j	iao	ˋ	jiào	wǒ jiào
	uang	ˊ	wáng	
j	ia	ˉ	jiā	
m	ing	ˊ	míng	wáng jiāmíng
d	a	ˋ	dà	
	uei	ˋ	wèi	dà wèi

2. Rules of the Chinese Phonetic Transcription (*Pinyin*).

(1) Special syllables

<table>
<tr><td rowspan="2">special syllables</td><td>syllables that contain liaison of the initial and the final</td><td>zi ci si</td><td colspan="2">zhi chi shi ri</td></tr>
<tr><td>syllables without initials (zero initials)</td><td>yi (-i)
ye (-ie)
yin (-in)
ying (-ing)</td><td>wu (-u)
wa (-ua)
wai (-uai)
wei (-uei)
wo (-uo)
wang (-uang)
weng (-ueng)</td><td>yu (-ü)
yun (-ün)
yue (-üe)
yuan (-üan)</td></tr>
</table>

(2) Tone sandhi

original tones	actual tones
nǐ + hǎo	ní hǎo When two characters of the third tone are joined together, the first one is pronounced with a second tone.

Can you sing it?

Chinese characters

Here are some examples of different kinds of Chinese characters. Can you spot the difference between each line of characters?

王	大	卫	我
你	好	明	叫
家			

2 再 见

zài jiàn

林老师：同学们好！ Lín lǎoshī: Tóngxuémen hǎo!

同学们：老师好！ Tóngxuémen: Lǎoshī hǎo!

林老师：同学们再见！ Lín lǎoshī: Tóngxuémen zàijiàn!

同学们：林老师再见！ Tóngxuémen: Lín lǎoshī zàijiàn!

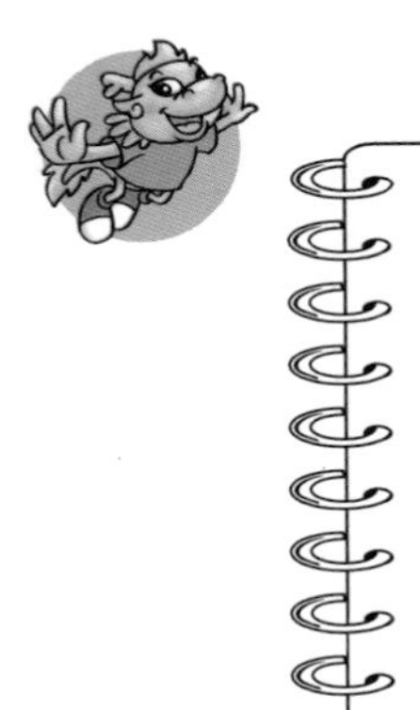

New words

1. 同学 tóngxué (n.) classmate ①
2. 们 men (suf.) suffix ②
3. 老师 lǎoshī (n.) teacher ③
4. 再见 zàijiàn (v.) see you; good-bye

Proper noun

- 林（老师）
  Lín (lǎoshī)
  a surname

Classroom Chinese

- Xiànzài shàng kè! Let's begin class.
- Xiànzài xià kè! Class is over.

Read, then practice with a partner.

---

① Here a form of address used in speaking to a student.

② Suffix used to form a plural number when added to a personal pronoun or a noun referring to a person (not used when the pronoun or noun is preceded by a numeral or an intensifier).

③ Here sir or madam.

④ See you tomorrow.

On your own: Connect the following people with what they say.

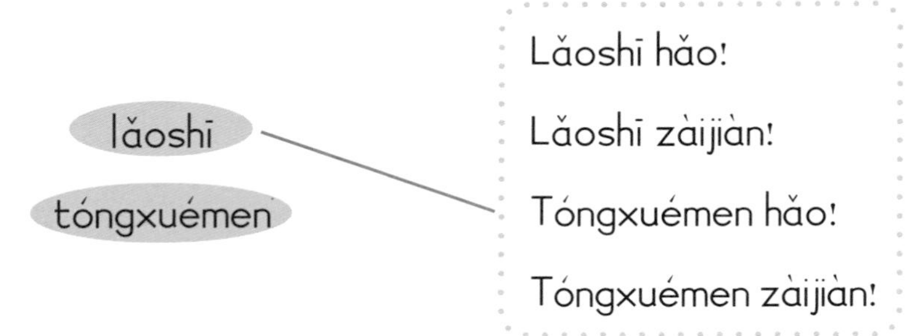

Class activity

1. Go around the room. Practice greeting classmates and then saying good-bye.
2. Make a Chinese paper pinwheel.

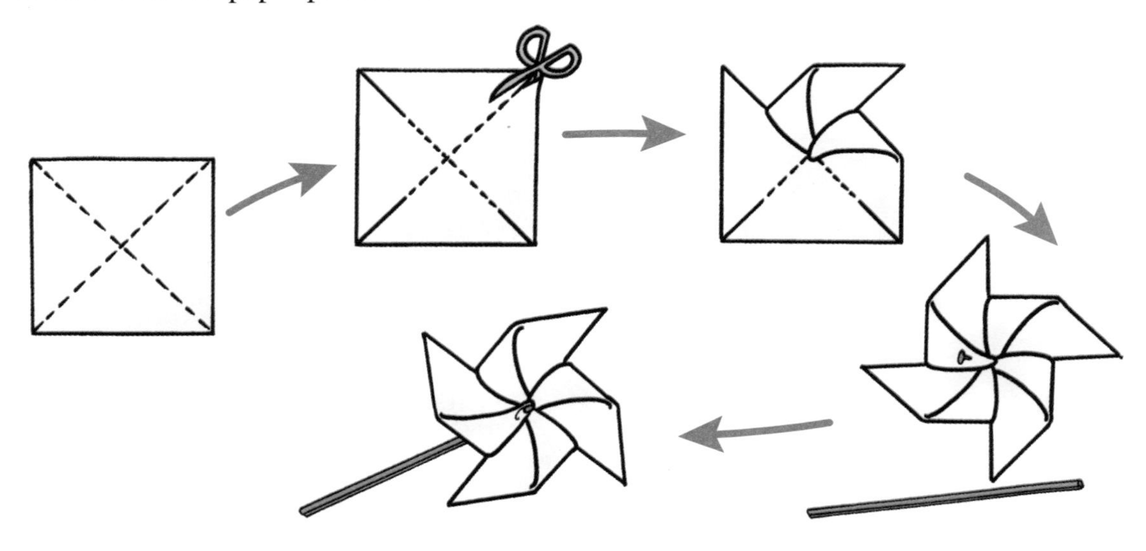

Phonetics

1. Listen to the tape, and then complete the following exercises.

(1) Write down the syllables (including the tones) you hear, and then read them out.

(2) Answer the following questions: Who is talking? What are they talking about?

2. The combinations of the initials b, p, m, f and the finals a, o, e. Read the combinations in four tones.

	a	ai	ao	an	ang	o	ou	e	ei	en	eng
b	ba	bai	bao	ban	bang	bo			bei	ben	beng
p	pa	pai	pao	pan	pang	po	pou		pei	pen	peng
m	ma	mai	mao	man	mang	mo	mou	me	mei	men	meng
f	fa			fan	fang	fo	fou		fei	fen	feng

3. **Listen to the tape, and then choose the syllables you hear.**

Chinese characters

Can you spot the difference between each line of Chinese characters?

再	见	
林	师	们
老	学	同

3 我是王家明
wǒ shì wáng jiā míng

Wang Jiaming comes to a biology class first time.

家　明：林老师好！
　　　　我是王家明。
林老师：你好！

Jiāmíng: Lín lǎoshī hǎo!
　　Wǒ shì Wáng Jiāmíng.
Lín lǎoshī: Nǐ hǎo!

The teacher groups Wang Jiaming, Mary and Jack together to conduct an experiment and now they get to know each other.

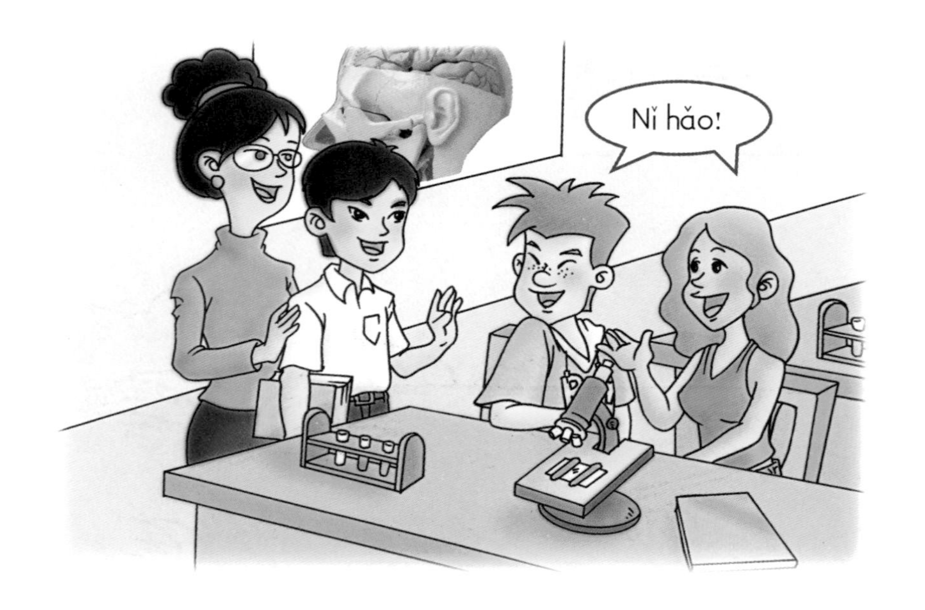

林老师：她是玛丽，
　　　　他是杰克。
家　明：你们好！
玛丽、杰克：你好！

Lín lǎoshī: Tā shì Mǎlì,
　　Tā shì Jiékè.
Jiāmíng: Nǐmen hǎo!
Mǎlì、Jiékè: Nǐ hǎo!

New words

1. 是	shì	(v.)	be(is/am/are)
2. 她	tā	(pron.)	she
3. 他	tā	(pron.)	he
4. 你们	nǐmen	(pron.)	you(plural)

Proper nouns

- 玛丽 Mǎlì Mary
- 杰克 Jiékè Jack

Classroom Chinese

- Qǐng gēn wǒ shuō! Please say it after me.

Read, then practice with a partner.

On your own: Practice introducing two friends to each other.

Nǐ hǎo, tā shì ________, tā ________.   Nǐ hǎo, tā shì ________, tā ________.

Class activity: Who are you?

Use a "fake" name to introduce yourself to your partner. See if he can guess who you are.

Phonetics

1. Listen to the tape, and then complete the following exercises.

(1) Write down the syllables (including the tones) you hear, and then read them out.

(2) Answer the following questions: How many people are talking? Who are they?

2. The combinations of the initials b, p, m, f **and the finals** i, u. **Read the combinations in four tones.**

	i	ie	iao	ian	in	ing	u
b	bi	bie	biao	bian	bin	bing	bu
p	pi	pie	piao	pian	pin	ping	pu
m	mi	mie	miao	mian	min	ming	mu
f							fu

3. **Listen to the tape, and then choose the syllables you hear.**

Learn to write

Can you spot the difference between each line of Chinese characters?

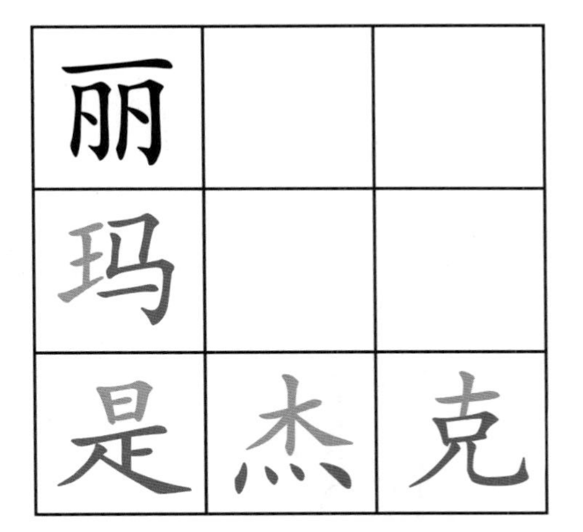

谢 谢
xiè xie

老师：谢谢你！
家明：不客气。

Lǎoshī: Xièxie nǐ!

Jiāmíng: Bú kèqi.

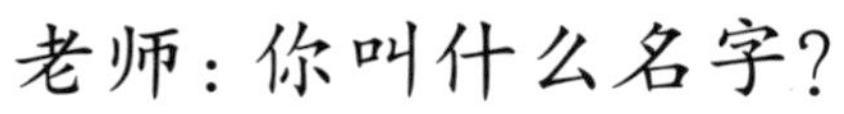

老师：你叫什么名字？
家明：我叫王家明。

Lǎoshī: Nǐ jiào shénme míngzi?

Jiāmíng: Wǒ jiào Wáng Jiāmíng.

家明：老师再见。
老师：再见。

Jiāmíng: Lǎoshī zàijiàn.

Lǎoshī: Zàijiàn.

New words

1. 谢谢	xièxie	(v.)	thank
2. 不客气	bú kèqi		You're welcome.
3. 什么	shénme	(pron.)	what
4. 名字	míngzi	(n.)	name

Classroom Chinese

- Qǐng kàn hēibǎn! Please look at the blackboard.

Read, then practice with a partner.

On your own: Complete the following sentences.

Nǐ hǎo, wǒ jiào Cathy. Nǐ jiào ________ ?

Nǐ hǎo, wǒ jiào Julia. Nǐ ________ ?

A: Xièxie!

B: ______________ .

A: ______________ !

B: Bú kèqi.

Class activity: Getting to know new friends.

The students walk casually around the classroom, pretending not to know each other, while the teacher taps the table, gradually increasing the tempo until coming to a sudden stop. The two students closest to each other must begin to introduce themselves.

Phonetics

1. Listen to the tape, and then complete the following exercises.

(1) Write down the syllables (including the tones) you hear, and then read them out.

(2) Answer this question: What are the persons in the two dialogues talking about?

2. The combinations of the initials d, t, n, l and the finals a, o, e. Read the combinations in four tones.

	a	ai	ao	an	ang	ou	ong	e	ei	en	eng
d	da	dai	dao	dan	dang	dou	dong	de	dei	den	deng
t	ta	tai	tao	tan	tang	tou	tong	te			teng
n	na	nai	nao	nan	nang	nou	nong	ne	nei	nen	neng
l	la	lai	lao	lan	lang	lou	long	le	lei		leng

3. Listen to the tape, and then choose the syllables you hear.

dǎ	nài	dāo	náng
tǎ	lài	tāo	láng
lā	dài	láo	táng

děi	nèn	dān	nóng
děng	néng	dāng	tóng
téng	lèng	tāng	lóng

4. Read the phrases below and pay attention to tone sandhi.

bù'ān
unease

bù lái
not to come

bù děng
not to await

bú yào
not to want

Learn to write

1. General introduction to Chinese characters

Chinese characters are a written language that transcribes spoken Chinese. Because they occupy a square shape, we call them "square-shaped characters". Each Chinese character is composed of several different strokes, and the number of strokes varies greatly with each different character. The Chinese character is one of the oldest writing systems in the world. During its long history, the shape they have taken has evolved continuously, but at the core it remains the same as when it was first invented.

2. The evolution of characters

甲骨文[1] jiǎ gǔ wén	金文[2] jīn wén	籀文[3] zhòu wén	小篆[4] xiǎo zhuàn	楷书[5] kǎi shū	
				繁体字[6] fán tǐ zì	简体字[7] jiǎn tǐ zì
[illegible]	[illegible]	[illegible]	[illegible]	人	人
[illegible]	[illegible]	[illegible]	[illegible]	魚	鱼
[illegible]	[illegible]	[illegible]	[illegible]	林	林
	[illegible]	[illegible]	[illegible]	國	国

① Inscriptions on shells & bones.
② Inscriptions on ancient bronze objects.
③ Ancient style of calligraphy, current in the Zhou Dynasty (11th century BC-256 BC).
④ An ancient style of calligraphy, adopted in the Qin Dynasty for the purpose of standardizing the Chinese script.
⑤ Regular script.
⑥ Traditional characters.
⑦ Simplified characters.

3. Structure of Chinese characters

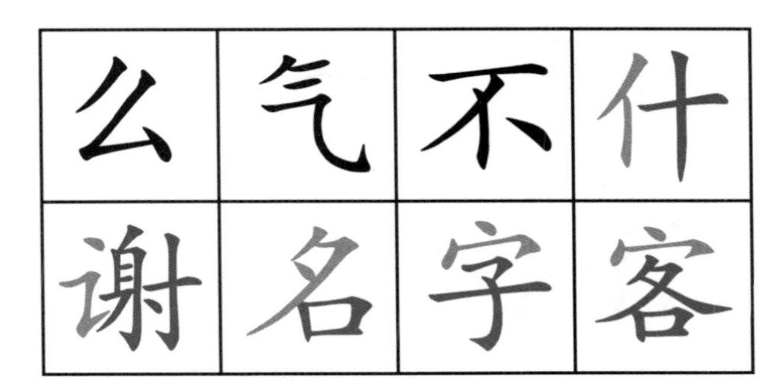

4. Strokes of Chinese characters

Since the Chinese character is made up of different strokes, we'd like to introduce you some of the basic strokes.

stroke pictures	丶	一	丨
names	diǎn dot stroke	héng horizontal line	shù vertical line
stroke directions	↘	→	↓
examples	家 丽	王 大	王 们

5. Tell the names of the following strokes.

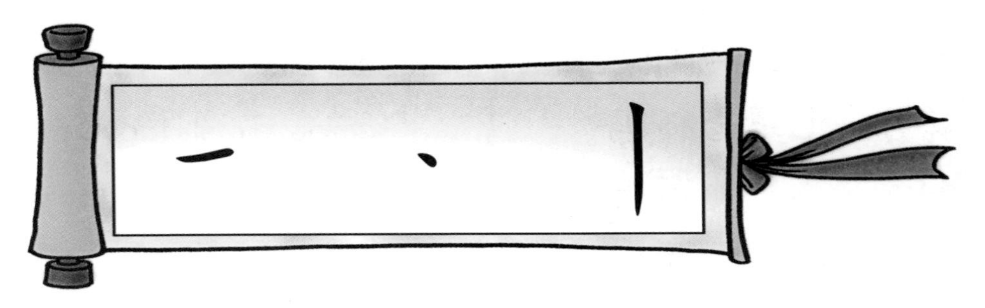

5 她们是学生吗

tā men shì xué sheng ma

At the school art festival, the principal is presenting awards after the girls finished their performance. Wang Jiaming is asking Jack who they are.

家明：她们是学生吗？	Jiāmíng: Tāmen shì xuésheng ma?
杰克：是，她们是学生。	Jiékè: Shì, tāmen shì xuésheng.
家明：他是老师吗？	Jiāmíng: Tā shì lǎoshī ma?
杰克：不，他不是老师， 他是校长。	Jiékè: Bù, tā bú shì lǎoshī, tā shì xiàozhǎng.

New words

1. 她们 tāmen (pron.) they; them (female)
2. 学生 xuésheng (n.) student
3. 吗 ma (pt.) particle word ①
4. 校长 xiàozhǎng (n.) headmaster; principal; (university or college) president

Classroom Chinese

- Qǐng dǎ kāi shū! Please open your books.

Read, then practice with a partner.

① Used at the end of a yes-no question.

On your own: Complete the following sentences.

A: Tāmen shì xuésheng ma?

B: Shì, ____________________.

A: Tā shì lǎoshī ma?

B: Shì, ____________________.

A: Tā shì xiàozhǎng ma?

B: Shì, ____________________.

A: Tāmen shì lǎoshī ma?

B: Bù, ____________________.

Class activity: Read my mind.

Write down the names of a teacher, a principal and a friend whom everyone is familiar with. Have a student choose one from the three, without telling anyone else. Have the other students try to guess which one the student has chosen.

the teacher's name	the principal's name	the friend's name

A: "Shì lǎoshī ma?" "Shì xiàozhǎng ma?" "Shì __________ ma? (the friend's name)"

B: "Shì, shì __________." " Bù, bú shì __________."

Phonetics

1. Listen to the tape, and then complete the following exercises.

(1) Write down the syllables (including the tones) you hear, and then read them out.

(2) Answer the following questions: What is the girl asking about? How does the boy respond?

2. The combinations of the initials d, t, n, l and the finals i, u, ü. Read the combinations in four tones.

	i	ie	iao	iou	ian	iang	in	ing	u	uei	uo	uan	uen	ü	üe
d	di	die	diao	diu	dian			ding	du	dui	duo	duan	dun		
t	ti	tie	tiao		tian			ting	tu	tui	tuo	tuan	tun		
n	ni	nie	niao	niu	nian	niang	nin	ning	nu		nuo	nuan		nü	nüe
l	li	lie	liao	liu	lian	liang	lin	ling	lu		luo	luan	lun	lü	lüe

3. Listen to the tape, and then choose the syllables you hear.

Learn to write

1. Structure of Chinese characters

Can you spot the difference between each line of Chinese characters?

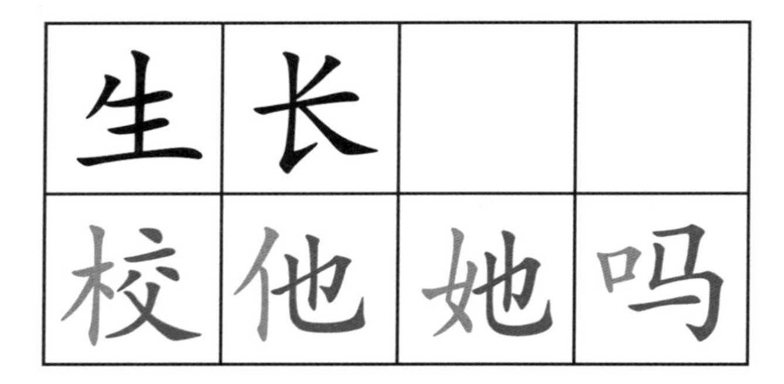

生	长		
校	他	她	吗

2. Strokes of Chinese characters

stroke pictures	丿	㇏	㇖
names	piě left-falling stroke	nà right-falling stroke	héng gōu horizontal line and a hook
stroke directions	↙	↘	→
examples	家 大	校 长	学 好

3. Tell the names of the following strokes.

6 他们是我的朋友

tā men shì wǒ de péng you

Jack and his classmates come to register themselves as volunteers for the community, and now he is introducing himself and his classmates to the staff member there.

你好，我叫杰克。他们是我的朋友，他叫王家明，她叫玛丽。我们是中学生。

Nǐ hǎo, wǒ jiào Jiékè. Tāmen shì wǒ de péngyou, tā jiào Wáng Jiāmíng, tā jiào Mǎlì. Wǒmen shì zhōngxuéshēng.

New words

1. 他们	tāmen	(pron.)	they; them (male)
2. 的	de	(pt.)	particle word ①
3. 朋友	péngyou	(n.)	friend
4. 我们	wǒmen	(pron.)	we; us
5. 中学生	zhōngxuéshēng	(n.)	high school student

① Used after an attribute, such as when the attribute is a personal pronoun or a name, as in the text.

Classroom Chinese

- Qǐng zài shuō yí biàn! Please say it again.

Read and match

他 tā

她 tā

他们 tā men

她们 tā men

On your own: Complete the following sentences.

A: Tāmen shì nǐ de péngyou ma?

B: Shì, ______________________ .

A: Tāmen shì nǐ de tóngxué ma?

B: Shì, ______________________ .

A: Tāmen shì nǐ de lǎoshī ma?

B: Shì, ______________________ .

A: Tāmen shì nǐ de péngyou ma?

B: Bù, ______________________ .

Class activity: Introduction.

Divide the class into several groups, each including 5-6 students. First have the students take turns introducing each other to the rest of the group, then have them choose one representative to introduce that group to the whole class.

Can you sing it?

Phonetics

1. Listen to the tape, and then complete the following exercises.

(1) Write down the syllables (including the tones) you hear, and then read them out.

(2) Answer the following questions: What's the teacher's surname? Whose friend is Mary? Are Tom and Emily college students?

2. Combinations of the initials and the finals.

(1) The combinations of the initials g, k, h, j, q, x and the finals u, ü. Read the combinations in four tones.

	u	ua	uai	ui	uo	uan	uen	uang	ü	üe	üan	ün
g	gu	gua	guai	gui	guo	guan	gun	guang				
k	ku	kua	kuai	kui	kuo	kuan	kun	kuang				
h	hu	hua	huai	hui	huo	huan	hun	huang				
j									ju	jue	juan	jun
q									qu	que	quan	qun
x									xu	xue	xuan	xun

(2) The combinations of the initials g, k, h, j, q, x and the final a, e, i. Read the combinations in four tones.

	a	ai	ao	an	ang	e	ei	en	eng	ou	ong	i	ia	ie	iao	iou	ian	iang	in	ing	iong
g	ga	gai	gao	gan	gang	ge	gei	gen	geng	gou	gong										
k	ka	kai	kao	kan	kang	ke	kei	ken	keng	kou	kong										
h	ha	hai	hao	han	hang	he	hei	hen	heng	hou	hong										
j												ji	jia	jie	jiao	jiu	jian	jiang	jin	jing	jiong
q												qi	qia	qie	qiao	qiu	qian	qiang	qin	qing	qiong
x												xi	xia	xie	xiao	xiu	xian	xiang	xin	xing	xiong

3. Listen to the tape, and then choose the syllables you hear.

Learn to write

1. Structure of Chinese characters

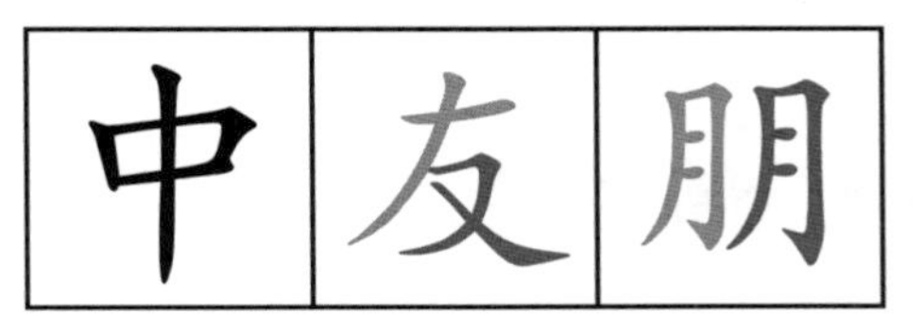

2. Strokes of Chinese characters

There are altogether 6 basic strokes in Chinese characters, but sometimes they also have variants. The following are some of the examples.

stroke pictures	亅	㇀	㇕	㇆
names	shù gōu vertical line with a hook	tí rising stroke	héng zhé horizontal line and then a turning	héng zhé gōu horizontal line and then a down turning with a hook
stroke directions	↓↖	↗	→↓	→↓↖
examples	你	我	明 叫	也 们

Unit Summary

Functional Usage

1. Greetings

你 好！
nǐ hǎo

您 好！
nín hǎo

你 们 好！
nǐ men hǎo

同 学 们 好！
tóng xué men hǎo

老 师 好！
lǎo shī hǎo

2. Expressing gratitude

谢 谢。
xiè xie

不 客 气！
bú kè qi

3. Saying farewell

再 见！
zài jiàn

4. Introducing oneself

我 叫……
wǒ jiào

我 是……
wǒ shì

5. Inquiring about others

你 叫 什 么 名 字？
nǐ jiào shén me míng zi

他 是 学 生 吗？
tā shì xué sheng ma

6. Introducing others

他 是……
tā shì

她 是……
tā shì

他 们 是……
tā men shì

她 们 是……
tā men shì

GRAMMAR FOCUS

Sentence pattern	Example
1. 你好 nǐ hǎo	你好！你们好！ nǐ hǎo nǐ men hǎo
2. 我叫…… wǒ jiào	我叫杰克。 wǒ jiào jié kè 我叫王家明。 wǒ jiào wáng jiā míng
3. 我是…… wǒ shì	我是学生。 wǒ shì xué sheng 我是老师。 wǒ shì lǎo shī
4. 是……吗？ shì ma	他是中学生吗？ tā shì zhōng xué shēng ma 他是校长吗？ tā shì xiào zhǎng ma
5. 不是…… bú shì	她不是学生。 tā bú shì xué sheng 他们不是中学生。 tā men bú shì zhōng xué shēng
6. ……的…… de	他们是我的朋友。 tā men shì wǒ de péng you 我是林老师的学生。 wǒ shì lín lǎo shī de xué sheng

STROKES OF CHINESE CHARACTERS

stroke pictures	*names*	*stroke directions*	*examples*
丶	diǎn dot stroke	↘	家 丽
一	héng horizontal line	→	王 大
丨	shù vertical line	↓	王 们
丿	piě left-falling stroke	↙	家 大
㇏	nà right-falling stroke	↘	校 长
㇖	héng gōu horizontal line and a hook	→	学 好
亅	shù gōu vertical line and a hook	↓↖	你
㇀	tí rising stroke	↗	我
㇕	héng zhé horizontal line and then a turning	→↓	明 叫
㇆	héng zhé gōu horizontal line and then a down turning with a hook	→↓↖	他 们

Unit Two

Hanging out with My Friends

Look and Say

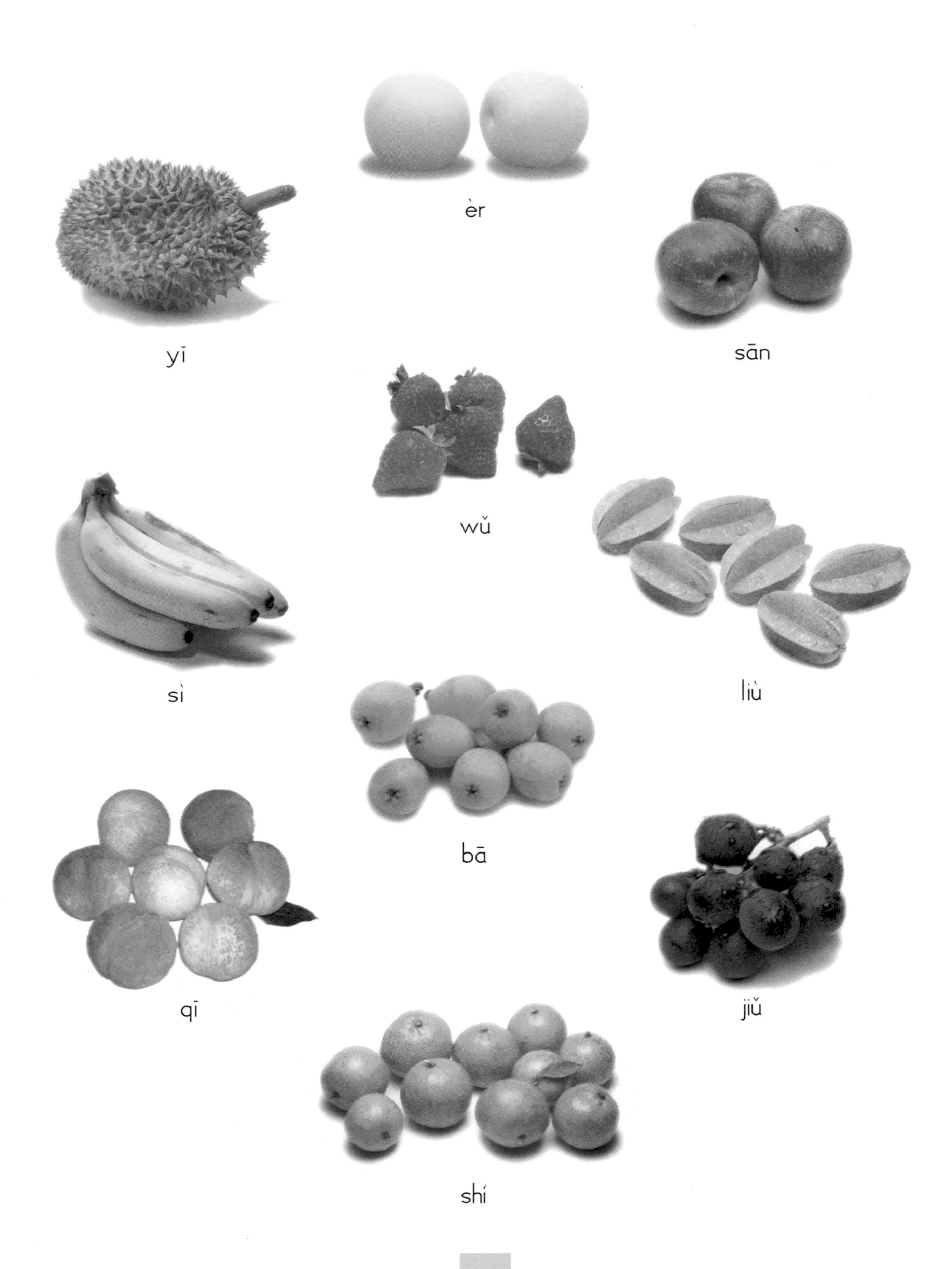
èr
yī
sān
wǔ
sì
liù
bā
qī
jiǔ
shí

7 他是谁

tā shì shuí

David is playing football when Wang Jiaming walks by, so David waves to him. The coach asks David something about Wang Jiaming.

教练：他是谁？
jiào liàn tā shì shuí

大卫：他是我的朋友王家明。
dà wèi tā shì wǒ de péng you wáng jiā míng

教练：他也打橄榄球吗？
jiào liàn tā yě dǎ gǎn lǎn qiú ma

大卫：不，他不打橄榄球，他打篮球。
dà wèi bù tā bù dǎ gǎn lǎn qiú tā dǎ lán qiú

New words

1. 教练	jiàoliàn	(n.)	coach; instructor
2. 谁	shuí	(pron.)	who
3. 也	yě	(adv.)	also; too
4. 打	dǎ	(v.)	play
5. 橄榄球	gǎnlǎnqiú	(n.)	American football
6. 篮球	lánqiú	(n.)	basketball

Classroom and daily Chinese

- Qǐng jìn! Please come in.
- Qǐng zuò! Please take a seat.
- Qǐng hē chá! Please have some tea.

Read aloud

dǎ wǎngqiú

dǎ yǔmáoqiú

dǎ bīngqiú

dǎ bàngqiú

dǎ pīngpāngqiú

dǎ páiqiú

On your own: Ask and answer questions based on the following pictures.

Example

A: Tā shì shuí?

B: Tā shì ________.

Conversation practice: Substitute the alternate words to make a new dialogue.

Example

A: Tā shì shuí?

B: Tā shì wǒ de péngyou Wáng Jiāmíng.

A: Tā yě dǎ wǎngqiú ma?

B: Shì, tā yě dǎ wǎngqiú.

1. Dàwèi	bàngqiú
2. Mǎlì	yǔmáoqiú
3. Líndá	páiqiú
4. Jiékè	bīngqiú

Class activity

Bring a picture of you and your friends and talk about what sports they like.

Tā shì shuí? Tā dǎ shénme qiú?

Phonetics

1. Listen to the tape, and then complete the following exercises.

(1) Write down the syllables (including the tones) you hear, and then read them out loud.

(2) Answer the following questions: Whose friend is Tom? What ball game does Tom play?

2. The combinations of initials, finals and tones.

(1) Pronounce the following syllables as a whole.

zhi	chi	shi	ri	zi	ci	si	er

(2) Combinations of initials zh, ch, sh, r, z, c, s and finals a, o. Read the combinations in four tones.

	a	ai	ao	an	ang	ou	ong
zh	zha	zhai	zhao	zhan	zhang	zhou	zhong
z	za	zai	zao	zan	zang	zou	zong
ch	cha	chai	chao	chan	chang	chou	chong
c	ca	cai	cao	can	cang	cou	cong
sh	sha	shai	shao	shan	shang	shou	
s	sa	sai	sao	san	sang	sou	song
r			rao	ran	rang	rou	rong

3. Listen to the tape, and then choose the syllables you hear.

Learn to write

1. Structure of Chinese characters

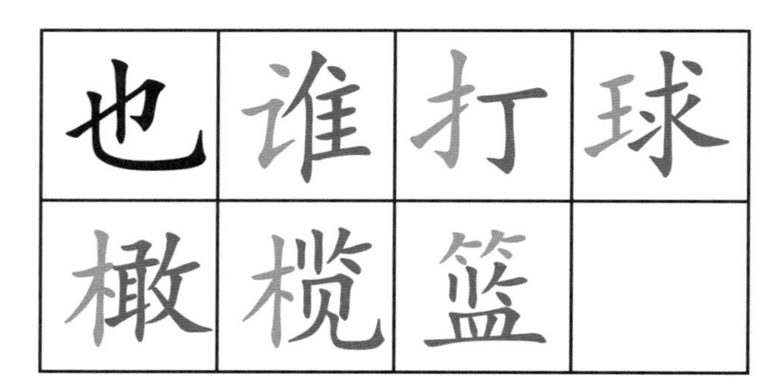

2. Stroke order of Chinese characters

Stroke order of Chinese character refers to the right order you should follow when writing a Chinese character. There are several rules for you to follow when writing different strokes.

(1) Horizontal line first, vertical line second; from top to bottom.

王	一	二	干	王							
打	一	十	扌	扌一	打						
客	丶	丷	冖	宀	宀丿	宀夕	宀夂	客	客		
家	丶	丷	冖	宀	宀一	宀丆	宀豕	宀豕	宀豕	家	
球	一	二	干	王	王一	玎	玎	玎	玎	球	球

(2) From left to right; the down stroke to the left before the one to the right.

大	一	ナ	大					
不	一	丆	不	不				
见	丨	冂	贝	见				
叫	丨	冂	口	口乚	叫			
林	一	十	木	木	木一	村	林	林

8 谁是你的好朋友
shuí shì nǐ de hǎo péng you

Wang Jiaming is talking with his father about his friends.

爸爸：家明，你有好朋友吗？
bà ba jiā míng nǐ yǒu hǎo péng you ma

家明：有啊。
jiā míng yǒu a

爸爸：谁是你的好朋友？
bà ba shuí shì nǐ de hǎo péng you

家明：大卫是我的好朋友，玛丽和艾米丽也是我的好朋友。
jiā míng dà wèi shì wǒ de hǎo péng you mǎ lì hé ài mǐ lì yě shì wǒ de hǎo péng you

爸爸：他们都学汉语吗？
bà ba tā men dōu xué hàn yǔ ma

家明：不，艾米丽不学汉语，她学法语。
jiā míng bù ài mǐ lì bù xué hàn yǔ tā xué fǎ yǔ

New words

1. 有	yǒu	(v.)	have
2. 啊	a	(pt.)	particle word ①
3. 都	dōu	(adv.)	both; all
4. 学	xué	(v.)	learn; study
5. 汉语	Hànyǔ	(n.)	the Chinese language
6. 法语	Fǎyǔ	(n.)	the French language

Proper noun

- 艾米丽

  Àimǐlì

  Emily

Classroom Chinese

- Qǐng ānjìng! Please be quiet.
- Qǐng tīng wǒ shuō! Please listen to me.

Read aloud: What language are they studying?

Hànyǔ

Yīngyǔ

Fǎyǔ

Rìyǔ

Xībānyáyǔ

① Softening the tone of the sentence, but adding no meaning to it when appearing at the end of it.

On your own: Look at the example and then ask and answer questions according to the pictures.

Example

shūbāo

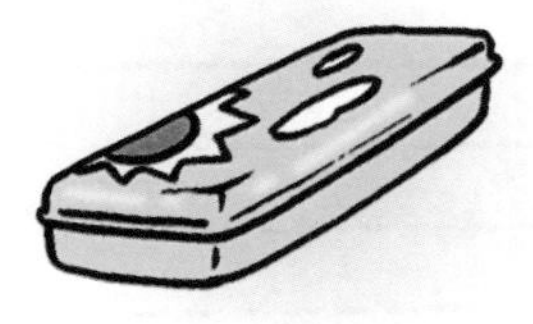

wénjùhé

qiānbǐ

Conversation practice: Substitute the alternate words to make a new dialogue.

Example

A: Nǐ yǒu hǎo péngyou ma?

B: Yǒu a. Wáng Jiāmíng shì wǒ de hǎo péngyou, Mǎlì yě shì wǒ de hǎo péngyou.

A: Tāmen dōu xué Hànyǔ ma?

B: Shì, tāmen dōu xué Hànyǔ.

1. Jim	Emma	xué Fǎyǔ
2. Bob	Stanley	xué Rìyǔ
3. Linda	Tom	dǎ lánqiú
4. Henry	Alice	dǎ wǎngqiú

Class activity

1. Possessions.

Make a list of your possessions, including classroom objects and personal items, then check with a partner.

A: Nǐ yǒu……ma?

B: Yǒu, wǒ yǒu……

(Méiyǒu, wǒ méiyǒu……)①

2. Let's make a Chinese paper fan!

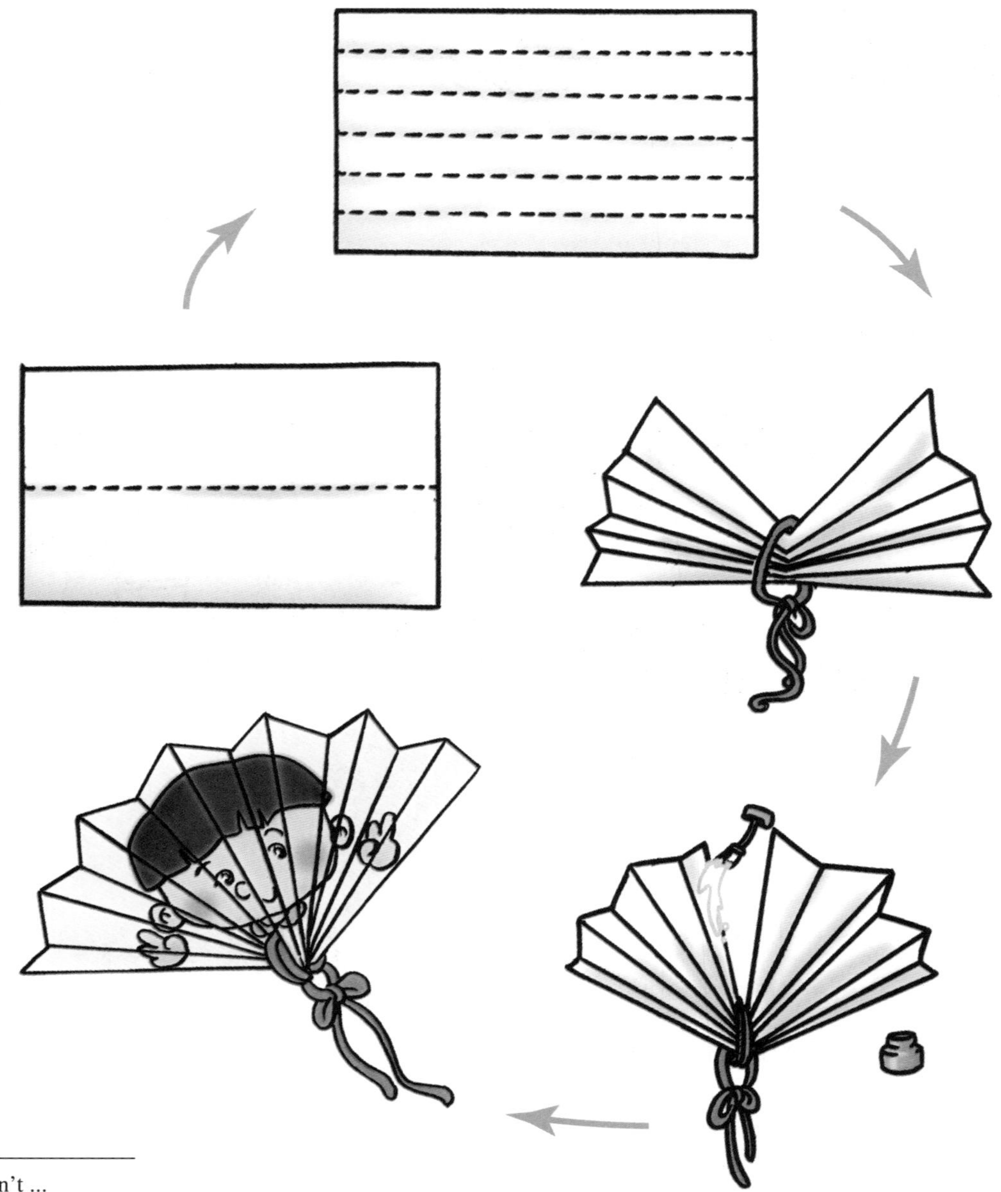

① I haven't ...

Phonetics

1. Listen to the tape, and then complete the following exercises.

(1) Write down the syllables (including the tone) you hear, and then read them.

(2) Answer the following questions: Does the boy have any good friends? Do the boy and his friends all study Chinese? Who doesn't study Chinese?

2. The combinations of initials zh, ch, sh, r, z, c, s, **and finals** e, u. **Read the combinations in four tones.**

	e	ei	en	eng	u	ua	uei	uai	uo	uan	uen	uang
zh	zhe	zhei	zhen	zheng	zhu	zhua	zhui	zhuai	zhuo	zhuan	zhun	zhuang
z	ze	zei	zen	zeng	zu		zui		zuo	zuan	zun	
ch	che		chen	cheng	chu	chua	chui	chuai	chuo	chuan	chun	chuang
c	ce		cen	ceng	cu		cui		cuo	cuan	cun	
sh	she	shei	shen	sheng	shu	shua	shui	shuai	shuo	shuan	shun	shuang
s	se		sen	seng	su		sui		suo	suan	sun	
r	re		ren	reng	ru		rui		ruo	ruan	run	

3. Listen to the tape, and then choose the syllables you hear.

cè　zhēn　zuǐ　zhuō

sè　shēn　shuǐ　chuō

rè　chén　ruǐ　shuō

zǔ　shū　zūn　cuàn

cū　shuā　chūn　zuàn

rǔ　shuāi　shùn　suàn

Learn to write

1. Structure of Chinese characters

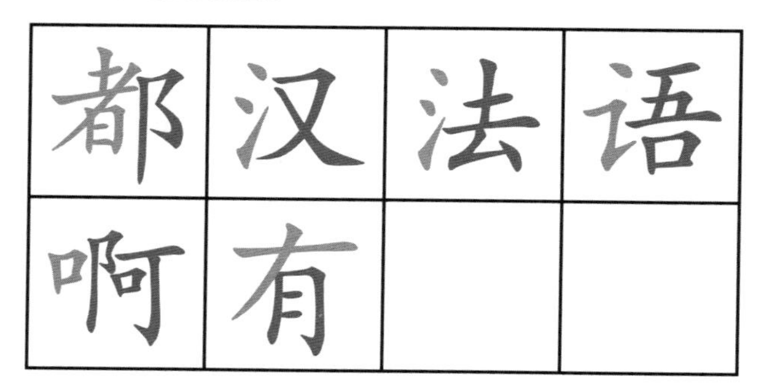

都	汉	法	语
啊	有		

2. Stroke order of Chinese characters

(1) Middle precedes the two sides

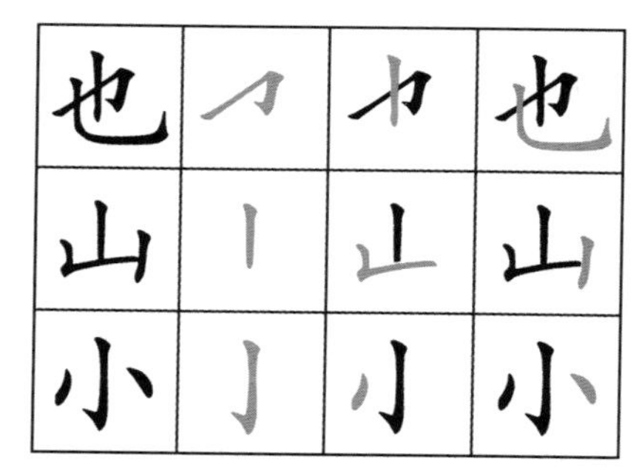

也	㇆	㐌	也
山	丨	凵	山
小	亅	小	小

(2) Inside precedes the sealing stroke

日	丨	冂	日	日
国	丨	冂	国	国

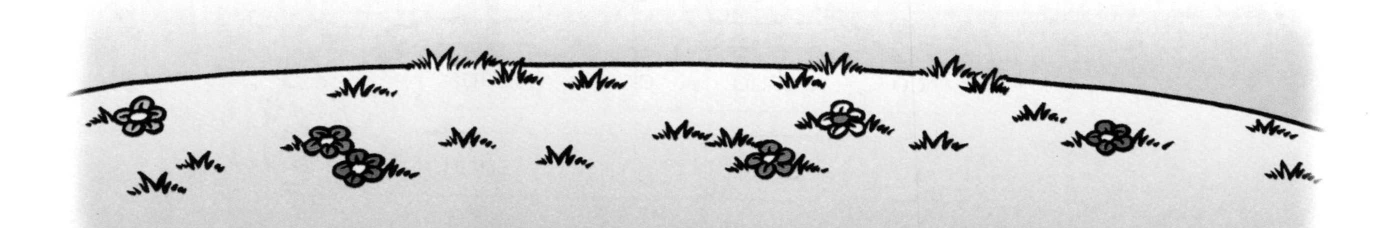

9 你有几张中文光盘

nǐ yǒu jǐ zhāng zhōng wén guāng pán

家明：大卫，你有几张中文光盘？
jiā míng dà wèi nǐ yǒu jǐ zhāng zhōng wén guāng pán

大卫：我有3张中文光盘。
dà wèi wǒ yǒu sān zhāng zhōng wén guāng pán

家明：杰克，你有几张？
jiā míng jié kè nǐ yǒu jǐ zhāng

杰克：我没有中文光盘。
jié kè wǒ méi yǒu zhōng wén guāng pán

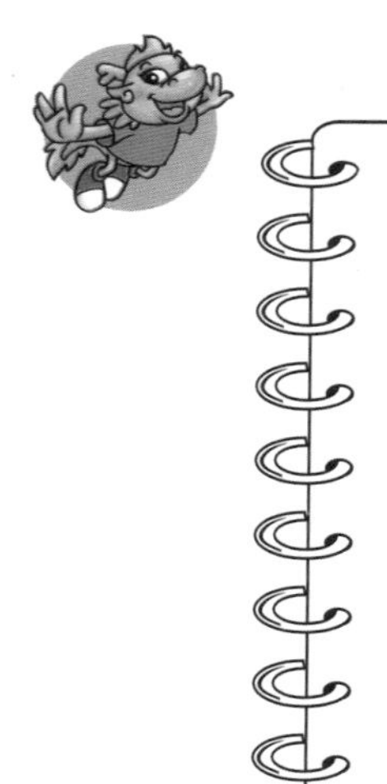

New words

1. 几	jǐ	(pron.)	how many
2. 张	zhāng	(m.)	measure word ①
3. 中文	Zhōngwén	(n.)	Chinese
4. 光盘	guāngpán	(n.)	disks; CDs
5. 没有	méiyǒu	(v.)	not to have; don't have

Classroom Chinese

- Qǐng jǔ shǒu! Please raise your hand.
- Shǒu fàng xià! Please put down your hand.

Can you count to ten on one hand?

1 yī

2 èr

3 sān

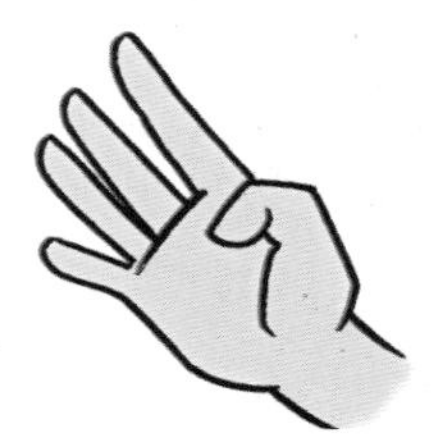

4 sì

5 wǔ

6 liù

7 qī

8 bā

9 jiǔ

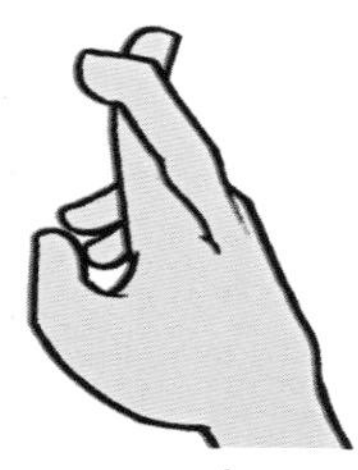

10 shí

---

① Used for disks, paper, tickets, etc.

On your own

1. Look at the example and then make conversations according to the pictures.

Example

2. Who has more? Give the results of the comparison.

Wǒ yǒu wǔ zhāng guāngpán.	Wǒ yǒu shí zhāng guāngpán.
Wǒ yǒu sān ge shūbāo.	Wǒ yǒu liǎng ge shūbāo.
Wǒ yǒu sì ge wénjùhé.	Wǒ yǒu bā ge wénjùhé.
Wǒ yǒu liù ge hǎo péngyou.	Wǒ yǒu yí ge hǎo péngyou.

Class activity

1. Telephone book: Make a list of names and phone numbers of classmates.

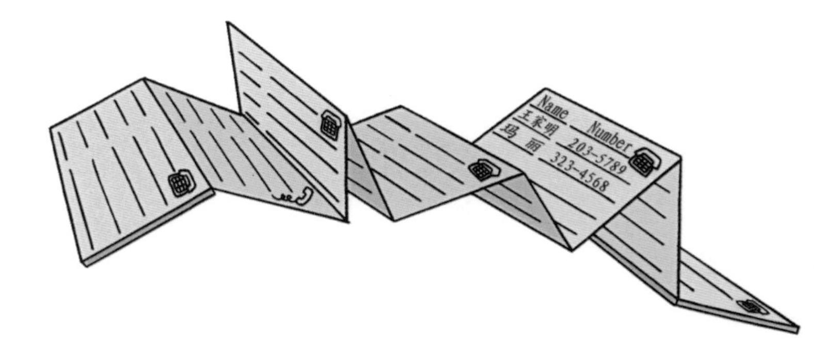

2. Flying chess of Chinese (see the appendix).

Phonetics

1. Listen to the tape, and then complete the following exercises.

(1) Write down the syllables you hear.

(2) Answer the following questions: How many students does Mrs. Lin have? How many Chinese disks does the boy have?

2. Read the phrases below and pay attention to the tone sandhi.

yì bēi

(a glass of …)

yì píng

(a bottle of …)

yì wǎn

(a bowel of …)

yí zuò

(a measure word for mountains etc.)

3. The comparison of combinations between zh, ch, sh, r **and** j, q, x**. Read the combinations in four tones.**

Initial \ Final	-i[ɿ,ʅ]	a	o	e	er	ai	ei	ao	ou	an	en	ang	eng	ong
j														
q														
x														
zh	zhi	zha		zhe		zhai	zhei	zhao	zhou	zhan	zhen	zhang	zheng	zhong
ch	chi	cha		che		chai		chao	chou	chan	chen	chang	cheng	chong
sh	shi	sha		she		shai	shei	shao	shou	shan	shen	shang	sheng	
r	ri			re				rao	rou	ran	ren	rang	reng	rong

Initial \ Final	i	ia	ie	iao	iou	ian	in	iang	ing	iong	u	ua	uo	uai
j	ji	jia	jie	jiao	jiu	jian	jin	jiang	jing	jiong				
q	qi	qia	qie	qiao	qiu	qian	qin	qiang	qing	qiong				
x	xi	xia	xie	xiao	xiu	xian	xin	xiang	xing	xiong				
zh											zhu	zhua	zhuo	zhuai
ch											chu	chua	chuo	chuai
sh											shu	shua	shuo	shuai
r											ru	rua	ruo	

4. Convert the following children's song into a rap.

一	只	青	蛙	一	张	嘴，
yì	zhī	qīng	wā	yì	zhāng	zuǐ
两	只	眼	睛	四	条	腿。
liǎng	zhī	yǎn	jing	sì	tiáo	tuǐ
两	只	青	蛙	两	张	嘴，
liǎng	zhī	qīng	wā	liǎng	zhāng	zuǐ
四	只	眼	睛	八	条	腿。
sì	zhī	yǎn	jing	bā	tiáo	tuǐ

One frog, one mouth, two eyes, four legs.
Two frogs, two mouths, four eyes, eight legs.

Learn to write

1. Structure of Chinese characters

几	光	文
张	没	盘

2. **Components of Chinese characters**

Some Chinese characters must be treated as a whole, that is to say, they cannot be torn apart any further, such as “王” “卫” and “大”;while others are made up of several components, that is to say, they can be further divided, such as “你” “明” “家” and “谢”。“你” → “亻” + “尔”; “明” → “日” + “月”; “家” → “宀” + “豕”; “谢” → “讠” + “身” + “寸”。

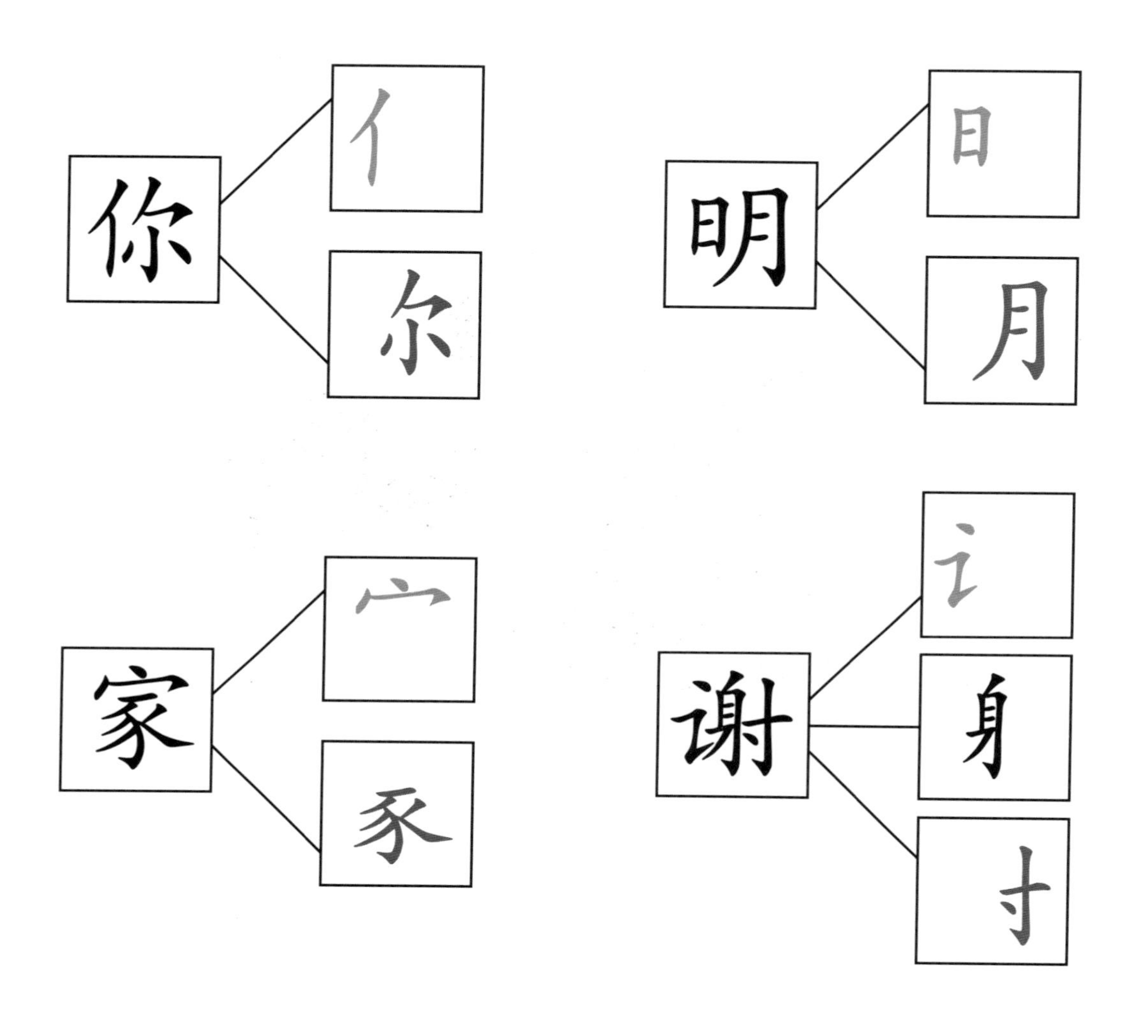

The smallest structure after the division is called components. There are many components, but now we will only introduce you a few of them.

3. Examples of components

部件 bù jiàn	甲骨文 jiǎ gǔ wén	金文 jīn wén	小篆 xiǎo zhuàn	楷书 kǎi shū	组字 zǔ zì
弓				弓	张
氵				水	没
口				口	叫
皿				皿	盘
亻				人	他

这是谁的钱包
zhè shì shuí de qián bāo

In the cafeteria, Wang Jiaming has just found a wallet on the floor.

店员：那是什么？
diàn yuán nà shì shén me

家明：是钱包！这是谁的钱包？
jiā míng shì qián bāo zhè shì shuí de qián bāo

女孩：是我的！
nǚ hái shì wǒ de

家明：钱包里有多少钱？
jiā míng qián bāo lǐ yǒu duō shao qián

女孩：38元钱。对吗？
nǚ hái sānshíbā yuán qián duì ma

家明：对，给你！
jiā míng duì gěi nǐ

女孩：谢谢你！
nǚ hái xiè xie nǐ

家明：不客气！
jiā míng bú kè qi

New words

1. 那	nà	(pron.)	that
2. 钱包	qiánbāo	(n.)	wallet; purse
3. 这	zhè	(pron.)	this
4. 里	lǐ	(n.)	in; inside
5. 多少	duōshao	(pron.)	how much; how many
6. 钱	qián	(n.)	money
7. 元	yuán	(m.)	measure word ①
8. 对	duì	(adj.)	yes; that's right ②
9. 给	gěi	(v.)	give

Classroom Chinese

- Hěn hǎo! Very good.
- Fēicháng hǎo! Very good. / Great.

Games of numbers

Did you know that you're already learned enough Chinese to count to 99?

1 2 3 4 5 6 7 8 9 10
11 12 13 14 15 16 17 18 19 20
21 22 23 24 25 26 ………… 30
31 32 33 34 35 ………… 40
41 42 43 44 ………… 50
51 52 53 ………… 60
61 62 ………… 70
71 ………… 80
81 ………… 90
91 ………… 100

a. Counting competition

Two people in a group take turns to count in Chinese. For instance, student A says "one", B "two", A "three", B "four" and so on and so forth until the number reaches one hundred. The faster one speaks, the better the game goes. After several practices, the entire class can have a timing competition in groups. The one that makes the fewest mistakes in the shortest time wins the game.

b. Neighboring numbers

The teacher will present a number, and the students will give the two neighboring numbers for that number. For example, if the teacher says "7", the students are supposed to say "6" and "8". The students can race to be the first to produce the right answers.

---

① Chinese monetary unit, similar to dollars.

② Here used for confirmation.

On your own

1. Complete the following sentences.

A: Zhè shì shénme?

B: Zhè shì ______________ .

A: Nà shì shénme?

B: Nà shì ______________ .

A: Zhè shì shénme?

B: _____ shì yì zhāng guāngpán.

A: Nà shì shénme?

B: _____ shì yì bǎi yuán qián.

2. Do the following calculations and read them out loud in Chinese.

20 + 35 = __________ 31 + 19 = __________

42 + 36 = __________ 45 + 55 = __________

Conversation practice: Substitute the alternate words to make a new dialogue.

Example

A: Zhè shì shuí de qiánbāo?

B: Zhè shì wǒ de qiánbāo.

C: Bù, zhè bú shì nǐ de, zhè shì wǒ de.

1. guāngpán	tā
2. shūbāo	Mǎlì
3. qiānbǐ	Jiékè

Class activity: Whose is it?

Have student split into groups of 5 ~ 6. One student should take a couple of the other students' pens, pencils, binders, etc, while they all keep their eyes closed. That student will then hold the items up one by one and have the other students guess whose it is.

A: Zhè shì shuí de wénjùhé?

B: Zhè shì wǒ de.

C: Bú duì. Zhè bú shì nǐ de,

zhè shì …… de.

D: Duì! Zhè shì wǒ de.

(The real owner should let the other students guess untill they figure out whose it is.)

Phonetics

1. Listen to the tape, and then complete the following exercises.

(1) Write down the syllables you hear.

(2) Answer the following questions: Is the wallet the girl's? How much money is there in the wallet? Is the sum of money the girl says right?

2. Listen to the tape, and then repeat what you hear. Pay attention to the tone sandhi.

3. Read the following tongue twister.

十 四 是 十 四，
shí sì shì shí sì

四 十 是 四 十。
sì shí shì sì shí

别 说 四 十 是 十 四，
bié shuō sì shí shì shí sì

别 说 十 四 是 四 十。
bié shuō shí sì shì sì shí

Fourteen is fourteen, forty is forty.
Don't say forty as fourteen.
Don't say fourteen as forty.

Learn to write

1. Structure of Chinese characters

里	少	元	多	对
给	钱	那	这	包

2. Examples of components

部件 bù jiàn	甲骨文 jiǎ gǔ wén	金文 jīn wén	小篆 xiǎo zhuàn	楷书 kǎi shū	组字 zǔ zì
钅		[illegible]	[illegible]	金	钱
女	[illegible]	[illegible]	[illegible]	女	她
子	[illegible]	[illegible]	[illegible]	子	好
门	[illegible]	[illegible]	[illegible]	门(門)	们

祝你生日快乐

zhù nǐ shēng ri kuài lè

12 o'clock at noon, the students are preparing for the celebration of Wang Jiaming's birthday in the classroom. They want to give him a surprise. However, when Wang Jiaming enters the classroom, there is only Mrs. Lin there.

王家明：林老师，您好！
wáng jiā míng lín lǎo shī nín hǎo

林老师：你找谁？
lín lǎo shī nǐ zhǎo shuí

王家明：我找大卫和玛丽。
wáng jiā míng wǒ zhǎo dà wèi hé mǎ lì

林老师：他们不在这里。
lín lǎo shī tā men bú zài zhè lǐ

王家明：他们在哪里？
wáng jiā míng tā men zài nǎ li

David, Jack and Mary enter the classroom with a birthday cake.

大卫、杰克、玛丽：
dà wèi jié kè mǎ lì

我们在这里！
wǒ men zài zhè lǐ

祝你生日快乐！
zhù nǐ shēng ri kuài lè

New words

1. 您	nín	(pron.)	polite form of "you" (singular)
2. 找	zhǎo	(v.)	to find; to look for
3. 和	hé	(conj.)	and
4. 在	zài	(v.)	be
5. 这里	zhèlǐ	(pron.)	here
6. 哪里	nǎli	(pron.)	where
7. 祝	zhù	(v.)	offer good wishes; wish
8. 生日	shēngri	(n.)	birthday
9. 快乐	kuàilè	(adj.)	happy; joyous

Read, then practice with a partner.

A: Jiékè hé Mǎlì zài nǎli?

B: Tāmen zài nàli.

A: Wǒ de wénjùhé zài nǎli?

B: Nǐ de wénjùhé zài zhèlǐ.

A: Wǒ de qiānbǐ zài nǎli?

B: Nǐ de qiānbǐ bú zài zhèlǐ.

A: Wǒ de qiánbāo zài nǎli?

B: Nǐ de qiánbāo bú zài zhèlǐ.

Conversation practice: Substitute the alternate words to make a new dialogue.

1.

A: Nǐ zhǎo shuí?

B: Wǒ zhǎo Wáng Jiāmíng hé Mǎlì

A: Tāmen bú zài zhèlǐ.

B: Tāmen zài nǎli?

A: Wǒ yě bù zhīdào.[①]

1. Emma	Linda
2. Jim	Sam
3. Wáng xiàozhǎng	Lín lǎoshī

2.

A: Nǐ zhǎo shénme?

B: Wǒ zhǎo qiánbāo.

A: Nǐ de qiánbāo zài zhèlǐ.

B: Xièxie nǐ!

A: Bú kèqi!

1. wénjùhé
2. qiānbǐ
3. Zhōngwén guāngpán

Class activity

Now let's make a birthday card in Chinese for the student whose birthday is coming soon.

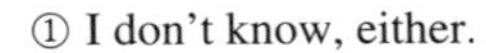

① I don't know, either.

Can you sing it?

Phonetics

1. Listen to the tape, and then complete the following exercises.

(1) Retell the story you hear.

(2) Answer these questions: Whom does the boy want to find? Did the boy find the person he was looking for?

2. Listen to the tape, and then repeat what you hear. Pay attention to the tone sandhi.

3. The following is a famous Chinese ancient poem. Can you follow the *Pinyin* to read it?

一 望 二 三 里，
yí wàng èr sān lǐ

烟 村 四 五 家。
yān cūn sì wǔ jiā

亭 台 六 七 座，
tíng tái liù qī zuò

八 九 十 枝 花。
bā jiǔ shí zhī huā

You can see two or three miles at one glance,
four or five houses with smoking chimneys.
Six or seven pavilions, and eight, nine or ten
flowers possibly.

Learn to write

1. Structure of Chinese characters

在	和	找	快
祝	哪	您	

2. Examples of components

部件 bù jiàn	甲骨文 jiǎ gǔ wén	金文 jīn wén	小篆 xiǎo zhuàn	楷书 kǎi shū	组字 zǔ zì
禾				禾	和
心				心	您
忄				心	快
扌				手	找
礻				示	祝
讠				言	谁

今天我很高兴

jīn tiān wǒ hěn gāo xìng

Diary

今天是我的生日。我跟朋友们在一起。我们吃蛋糕，听音乐。大家都很高兴，我也很高兴。

Jīntiān shì wǒ de shēngri. Wǒ gēn péngyoumen zài yìqǐ. Wǒmen chī dàngāo, tīng yīnyuè. Dàjiā dōu hěn gāoxìng, wǒ yě hěn gāoxìng.

New words

1. 今天	jīntiān	(n.)	today
2. 跟	gēn	(prep.)	with
3. 一起	yìqǐ	(n.)	together
4. 吃	chī	(v.)	eat; have
5. 蛋糕	dàngāo	(n.)	cake
6. 听	tīng	(v.)	listen (to)
7. 音乐	yīnyuè	(n.)	music
8. 大家	dàjiā	(pron.)	all, everybody
9. 很	hěn	(adv.)	very
10. 高兴	gāoxìng	(adj.)	happy; glad; cheerful

Classroom Chinese

- Qǐng dàshēng shuō! Please say it louder!

On your own: Match the following food with their *Pinyin*.

dàngāo

mǐfàn (boiled rice)

bǐsàbǐng (pizza)

qiǎokèlì (chocolate)

Conversation practice: Substitute the alternate words to make a new dialogue.

1. A: Jīntiān shì shuí de shēngri?

B: Jīntiān shì Jiāmíng de shēngri. Wǒmen chī dàngāo, tīng yīnyuè. Jiāmíng hěn gāoxìng, dàjiā dōu hěn gāoxìng.

1. Jim
2. Lín lǎoshī
3. Wáng xiàozhǎng

2. A: Nǐ gēn shuí zài yìqǐ?

B: Wǒ gēn péngyoumen zài yìqǐ. Wǒmen dōu hěn gāoxìng.

1. bàba
2. lǎoshīmen
3. lǎoshī hé tóngxuémen

Can you sing it?

Phonetics

1. Listen to the tape, and then complete the following exercises.

(1) Retell the story you hear.

(2) Answer these questions: Who is having a birthday today? Who is very happy today? Whom is Mary with today? What does Mary do with her friends today?

2. Listen to the tape, and then repeat what you hear. Pay attention to the tone sandhi.

3. Read the following children's song in Chinese.

一 闪 一 闪 亮 晶 晶，
yì shǎn yì shǎn liàng jīng jīng

满 天 都 是 小 星 星，
mǎn tiān dōu shì xiǎo xīng xing

挂 在 天 上 放 光 明，
guà zài tiān shang fàng guāng míng

好 像 许 多 小 眼 睛。
hǎo xiàng xǔ duō xiǎo yǎn jing

Learn to write

1. Structure of Chinese characters

今	天	日	一	乐
起	吃	听	很	糕
蛋	音	兴	高	

2. Examples of components

部件 bù jiàn	甲骨文 jiǎ gǔ wén	金文 jīn wén	小篆 xiǎo zhuàn	楷书 kǎi shū	组字 zǔ zì
走				走	起
米				米	糕
木				木	林
又				又	友
日				日	明

UNIT SUMMARY

FUNCTIONAL USAGE

1. Inquiring about someone's identity

他 是 谁?
tā shì shuí

2. Talking about friends

你 有 好 朋 友 吗?
nǐ yǒu hǎo péng you ma
谁 是 你 的 好 朋 友?
shuí shì nǐ de hǎo péng you

3. Inquiring about the quantity of certain things

你 有 几 张 中 文 光 盘?
nǐ yǒu jǐ zhāng zhōng wén guāng pán
钱 包 里 有 多 少 钱?
qián bāo lǐ yǒu duō shao qián

4. Inquiring about the owner

这 是 谁 的 钱 包?
zhè shì shuí de qián bāo

5. Looking for someone

他 们 在 哪 里?
tā men zài nǎ li

6. Expressing one's mood and feelings

今 天 我 很 高 兴。
jīn tiān wǒ hěn gāo xìng

GRAMMAR FOCUS

	Sentence pattern	Example
1.	……是 谁 shì shuí	他 是 谁? tā shì shuí
2.	……（没）有…… méi yǒu	我 有 好 朋 友。 wǒ yǒu hǎo péng you 我 没 有 好 朋 友。 wǒ méi yǒu hǎo péng you
3.	几…… jǐ	你 有 几 张 中 文 光 盘? nǐ yǒu jǐ zhāng zhōng wén guāng pán 我 有 6 张 中 文 光 盘。 wǒ yǒu liù zhāng zhōng wén guāng pán
4.	谁 的…… shuí de	这 是 谁 的 钱 包? zhè shì shuí de qián bāo
5.	……有 多 少…… yǒu duō shao	钱 包 里 有 多 少 钱? qián bāo lǐ yǒu duō shao qián
6.	……在…… zài	他 们 在 这 里。 tā men zài zhè lǐ 他 们 不 在 这 里。 tā men bú zài zhè lǐ
7.	……和…… hé	大 卫 和 玛 丽 在 哪 里? dà wèi hé mǎ lì zài nǎ li
8.	跟……在 一 起 gēn zài yì qǐ	我 跟 同 学 们 在 一 起。 wǒ gēn tóng xué men zài yì qǐ
9.	……很 高 兴 hěn gāo xìng	玛 丽 很 高 兴。 mǎ lì hěn gāo xìng
10.	……也…… yě	王 家 明 也 很 高 兴。 wáng jiā míng yě hěn gāo xìng
11.	……都…… dōu	我 们 都 很 高 兴。 wǒ men dōu hěn gāo xìng

STROKE ORDER OF CHINESE CHARACTERS

stroke order of Chinese characters	*examples*
(1) Horizontal precedes crossing vertical or down-stroke.	王 大 十
(2) From top to bottom.	三 客 家
(3) From left to right.	你 打 球
(4) Middle precedes the two sides.	小 水
(5) From outside to inside.	日 月 同
(6) Inside precedes the sealing stroke.	日 国

Unit Three

My Family and I

Look and Say

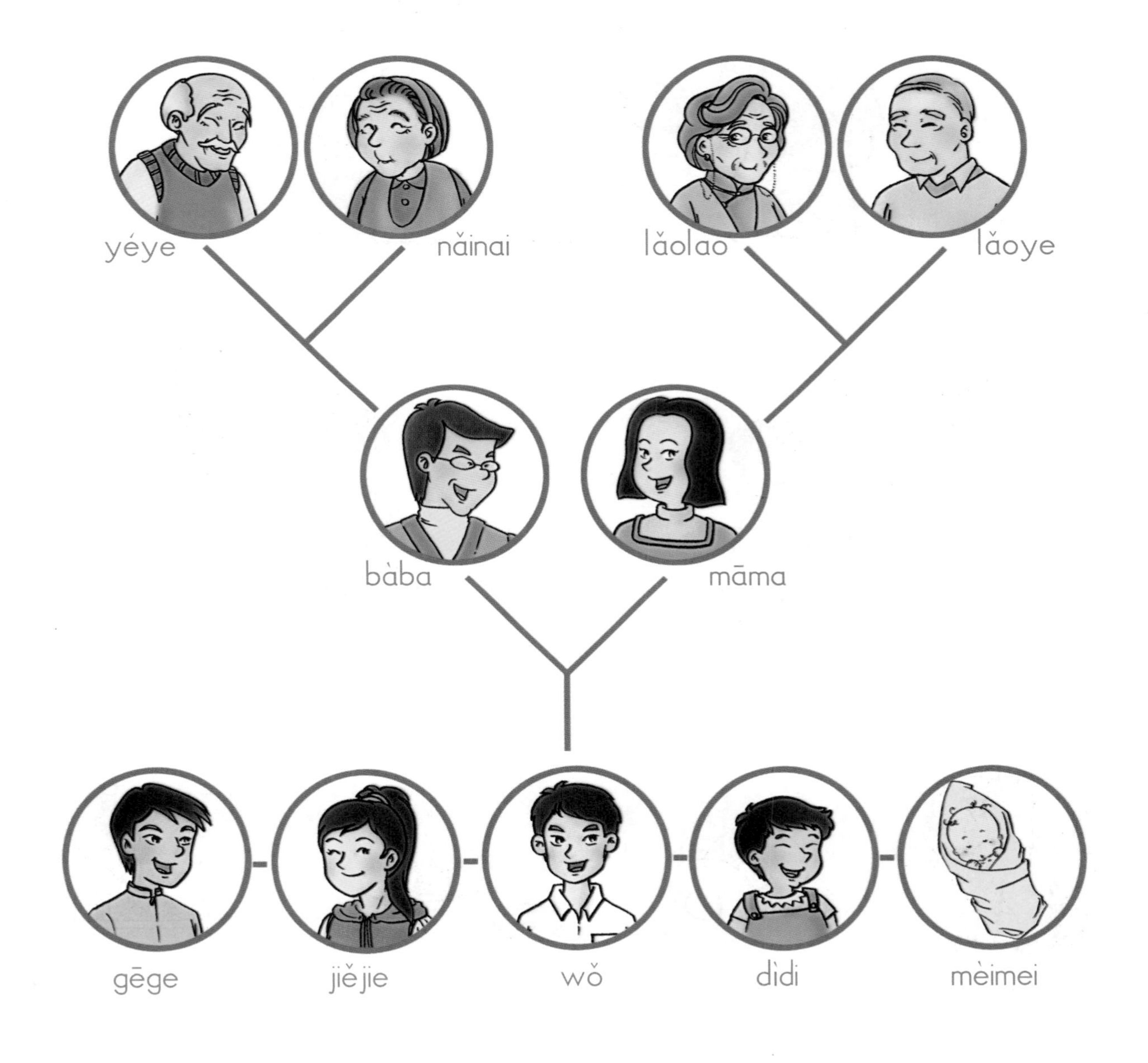

yì zhī gǒu

liǎng zhāng guāngpán

sān kuài qián

sì kǒu rén

13 你 多 大
nǐ duō dà

David and Wang Jiaming are reading an advertisement for a driving training course.

家 明：大 卫，你 多 大？
jiā míng dà wèi nǐ duō dà

大 卫：我 15 岁。
dà wèi wǒ shí wǔ suì

家 明：你 学 不 学 开 车？
jiā míng nǐ xué bu xué kāi chē

大 卫：当 然。你 呢，你 是 不 是 14 岁？
dà wèi dāng rán nǐ ne nǐ shì bu shì shí sì suì

家 明：对，我 14 岁。
jiā míng duì wǒ shí sì suì

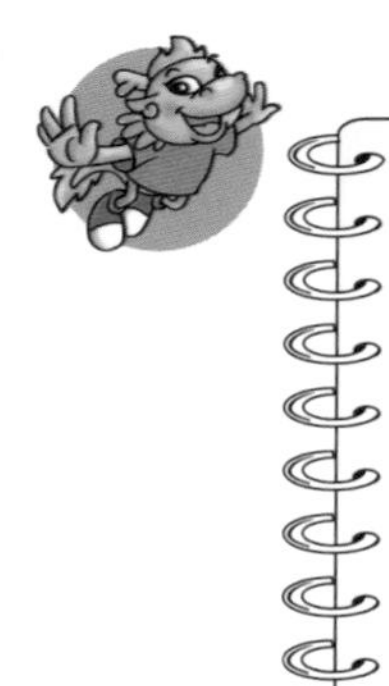

New words

1. 多大 duō dà how old
2. 岁 suì (m.) year (of age)
3. 开车 kāichē (v.) drive
4. 当然 dāngrán (adv.) certainly; of course

On your own: Ask and answer questions based on the following pictures.

A: 他 是 不 是 老 师?
tā shì bu shì lǎo shī

B: 是，他 是 老 师。
shì tā shì lǎo shī

他 中 学 生
tā zhōng xué shēng

她 们 好 朋 友
tā men hǎo péng you

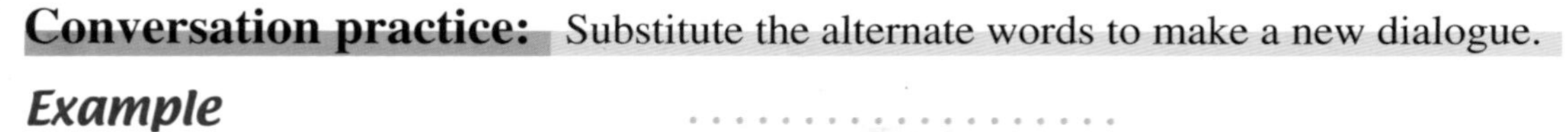

Conversation practice: Substitute the alternate words to make a new dialogue.

Example

A: Jim，你 多 大?
nǐ duō dà

B: 我 15 岁。
wǒ shí wǔ suì

A: 你 学 不 学 开 车?
nǐ xué bu xué kāi chē

B: 当 然。你 呢?
dāng rán nǐ ne

A: 我 14 岁，我 不 学 开 车。
wǒ shí sì suì wǒ bù xué kāi chē

1.	Sam	16
2.	Linda	17
3.	Robert	18

Class activity

1. Do you want to know more about your classmates? Take a survey and find out how old they are, then make a pie chart with the results.

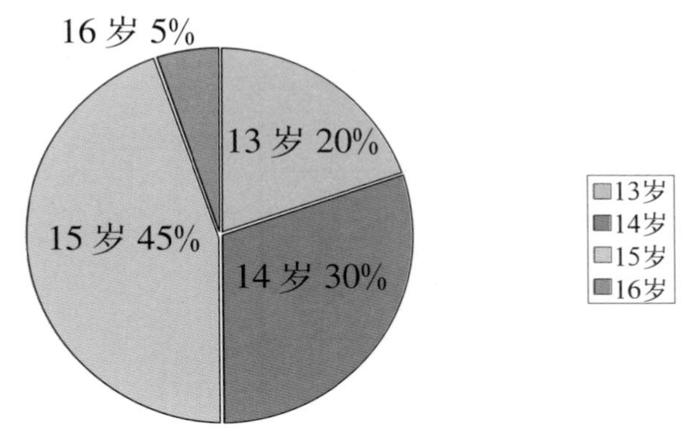

2. Discussion:

Do you like driving? What do you think are the advantages and the disadvantages of driving a car? How old do you think the proper age is for driving?

Phonetics

1. Listen to the tape, and then complete the following exercises.

(1) Retell what you hear.

(2) Answer these questions: How old is the boy who speaks first? How old is Jack? Is Jack going to learn driving? Is the boy who speaks first going to learn driving?

2. Read aloud the following children's song.

两 只 老 虎，两 只 老 虎，
liǎng zhī lǎo hǔ liǎng zhī lǎo hǔ

跑 得 快！跑 得 快！
pǎo de kuài pǎo de kuài

一 只 没 有 耳 朵，
yì zhī méi yǒu ěr duo

一 只 没 有 尾 巴，
yì zhī méi yǒu wěi ba

真 奇 怪！真 奇 怪！
zhēn qí guài zhēn qí guài

Two tigers are running fast. One has no ears, the other has no tail. How strange!

Learn to write

1. Structure of Chinese characters

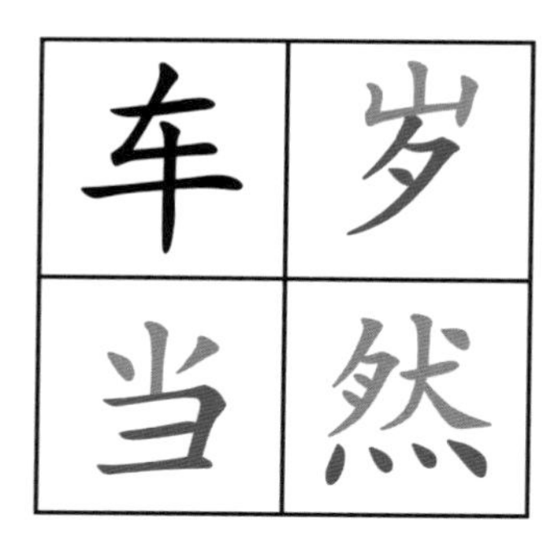

2. Examples of components

部件 bù jiàn	甲骨文 jiǎ gǔ wén	金文 jīn wén	小篆 xiǎo zhuàn	楷书 kǎi shū	组字 zǔ zì
灬				火	然 杰
寸				寸	对 谢
月				月	朋
交				交	校

14 这是我的狗
zhè shì wǒ de gǒu

Mary runs into Wang Jiaming when she is walking her dog.

家明：这是你的狗吗？
jiā míng zhè shì nǐ de gǒu ma

玛丽：对，是我的狗。
mǎ lì duì shì wǒ de gǒu

家明：它叫什么名字？
jiā míng tā jiào shén me míng zi

玛丽：它叫大黄。
mǎ lì tā jiào dà huáng

家明：它很漂亮。它几岁？
jiā míng tā hěn piào liang tā jǐ suì

玛丽：它两岁。
mǎ lì tā liǎng suì

New words

1. 狗 gǒu (n.) dog
2. 它 tā (pron.) it
3. 漂亮 piàoliang (adj.) pretty
4. 两 liǎng (num.) two

Proper noun

- 大黄 Dàhuáng Big Yellow (usually a name for a dog or a cat)

Learn to write numbers in Chinese.

yī 一　èr 二　sān 三　sì 四　wǔ 五

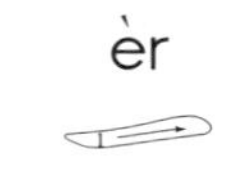

liù 六　qī 七　bā 八　jiǔ 九　shí 十

On your own: Ask and answer questions based on the following pictures.

A: 它 几 岁?
tā jǐ suì

B: 它 一 岁。
tā yí suì

八 岁
bā suì

四 岁
sì suì

A: 它 漂 亮 不 漂 亮?
tā piào liang bu piào liang

B: 它 很 漂 亮。
tā hěn piào liang

也 很 漂 亮
yě hěn piào liang

不 漂 亮
bú piào liang

Class activity

Interview your classmates:

1. Nǐ yǒu chǒngwù(pet) ma?
2. Nǐ yǒu shénme chǒngwù?
3. Tā jiào shénme míngzi?
4. Tā jǐ suì?(Tā duō dà?)
5. Tā piàoliang bu piàoliang?

Pets Survey

编号 number	同学姓名 classmate names	你有宠物吗? Do you have a pet?	什么宠物? What pet?	它叫什么名字? What's its name?	它几岁? How old is it?	它漂亮不漂亮? Is it pretty?
1.	玛丽	有	一只狗	大黄	两岁	很漂亮
2.	杰克	有	两只狗	黄黄、牛牛	一岁、三岁	都很漂亮
3.	王家明	没有				
4. ⋮						

Phonetics

1. Listen to the tape, and then answer the following questions.

(1) Does the dog belong to the boy or to the girl?
(2) How old is the dog?
(3) Does the boy think the dog is pretty?

2. Read aloud the following children's song.

宽 宽 一 条 河，河 上 一 群 鹅，
kuān kuān yì tiáo hé hé shang yì qún é

牧 鹅 一 少 年，口 中 唱 山 歌。
mù é yí shào nián kǒu zhōng chàng shān gē

On a wide river, geese are sporting. Among them is the herdboy. A folk song he is singing.

Learn to write

1. Structure of Chinese characters

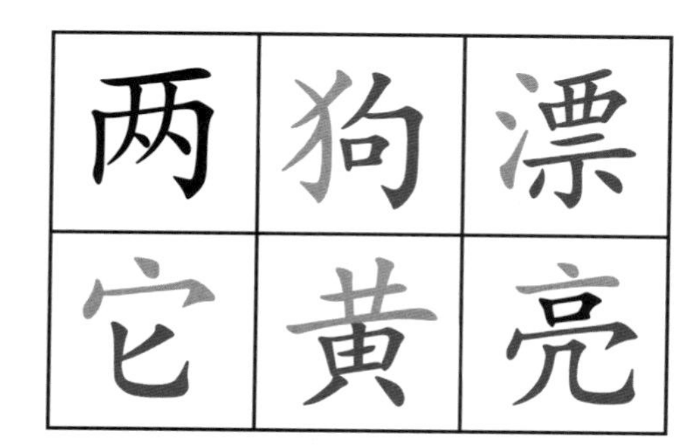

2. Examples of components

部件 bù jiàn	甲骨文 jiǎ gǔ wén	金文 jīn wén	小篆 xiǎo zhuàn	楷书 kǎi shū	组字 zǔ zì
犭				犬	狗
阝				阝(邑)	都
匕				匕	它
马				马(馬)	玛 吗
⺮				竹	篮
也				也	他 她

15 你从哪里来

nǐ cóng nǎ li lái

Mary is talking with her new neighbor in the yard.

玛丽：你好，你叫什么名字？
mǎ lì nǐ hǎo nǐ jiào shén me míng zi

邻居：我姓本田，我叫本田和美。你呢？
lín jū wǒ xìng běn tián wǒ jiào běn tián hé měi nǐ ne

玛丽：我叫玛丽。你从哪里来？
mǎ lì wǒ jiào mǎ lì nǐ cóng nǎ li lái

邻居：我从日本来。欢迎你来我家玩！
lín jū wǒ cóng rì běn lái huān yíng nǐ lái wǒ jiā wán

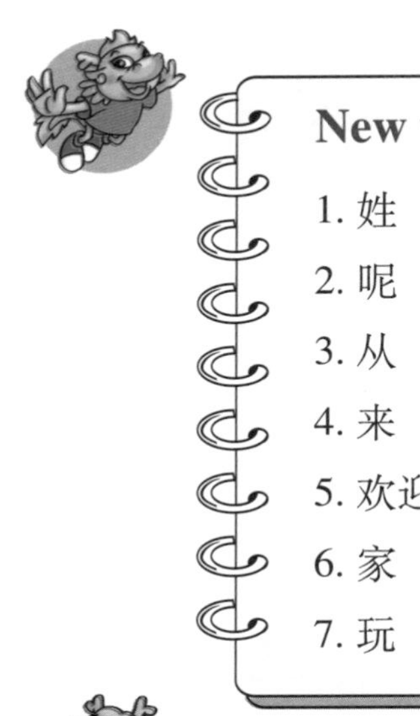

New words

1. 姓 xìng (v.) to be surnamed; surname
2. 呢 ne (pt.) particle word ①
3. 从 cóng (prep.) from
4. 来 lái (v.) come
5. 欢迎 huānyíng (v.) welcome
6. 家 jiā (n.) home
7. 玩 wán (v.) play

Proper noun

- 日本 Rìběn
  Japan

Read, then practice with a partner.

① Used at the end of an interrogative sentence here referring to the same content mentioned above.

Conversation practice: Substitute the alternate words to make a new dialogue.

Example

A: 你 姓 什 么?
nǐ xìng shén me

B: 我 姓 本 田。
wǒ xìng běn tián

A: 你 从 哪 里 来?
nǐ cóng nǎ li lái

B: 我 从 日 本 来。
wǒ cóng rì běn lái

1. 王 wáng	中国 zhōng guó
2. Miller	加拿大 jiā ná dà
3. Black	英国 yīng guó
4. Devinat	法国 fǎ guó

Class activity: Tracing your family's roots.

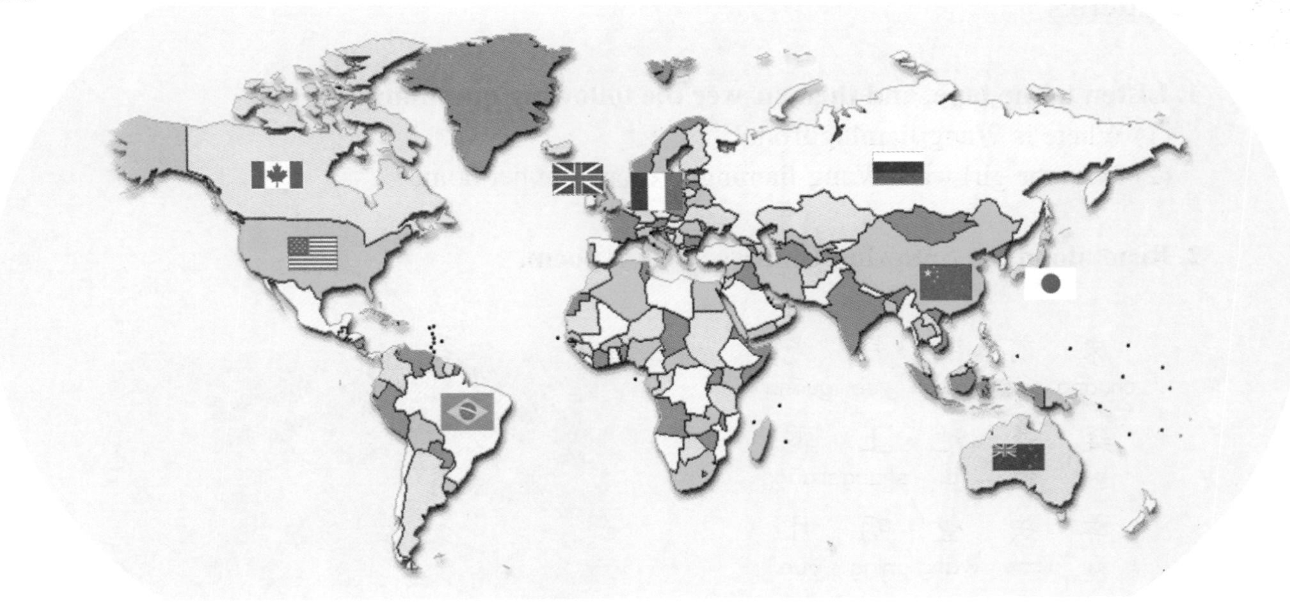

1. Ask your classmates:

Nǐ cóng nǎli lái?
Nǐ de bàba、māma cóng nǎli lái?
Tāmen jiào shénme míngzi?
Nǐ de yéye、nǎinai、lǎoye、lǎolao cóng nǎli lái?
Tāmen jiào shénme míngzi?

爸爸	bàba	father
妈妈	māma	mother
爷爷	yéye	grandfather, on father's side
奶奶	nǎinai	grandmother, on father's side
姥爷	lǎoye	grandfather, on mother's side
姥姥	lǎolao	grandmother, on mother's side

2. Try to identify which is the family name and which is the given name for each of the names listed below. Can you tell the difference between the western and Chinese names?

Western names	Chinese names
David Alan Miller	Qián Jié (钱杰)
Susan Black	Lǐ Jiāměi (李家美)
William Taylor	Lín Měiyuè (林美月)
Bobby Lee Davis	Wáng Jiāmíng (王家明)
Charlotte Baubion	Wáng Yuèyue (王月月)

Phonetics

1. Listen to the tape, and then answer the following questions.

(1) Where is Wang Jiaming from?

(2) Does the girl want Wang Jiaming to drop in at her home?

2. Read aloud the following Chinese ancient poem.

床 前 明 月 光，
chuáng qián míng yuè guāng

疑 是 地 上 霜。
yí shì dì shang shuāng

举 头 望 明 月，
jǔ tóu wàng míng yuè

低 头 思 故 乡。
dī tóu sī gù xiāng

I wake and moonbeams play around my bed.
Glittering like hoarfroast to my wondering eyes.
Upwards the glorious moon I raise my head.
Then lay me down and thoughts of home arise.

Learn to write

1. Structure of Chinese characters

来	姓	欢
从	玩	迎

2. Examples of components

部件 bù jiàn	甲骨文 jiǎ gǔ wén	金文 jīn wén	小篆 xiǎo zhuàn	楷书 kǎi shū	组字 zǔ zì
生				生	姓
人				人	从
欠				欠	欢
𤣩		王	王	玉	玩
丩				丩	叫
𠂇				𠂇	友 有

16 我住在柏树街
wǒ zhù zài bǎi shù jiē

Wang Jiaming is calling Pizza Hut to order a pizza.

店　员：喂，比 萨 饼 店。请 问，您 要 什 么？
diàn yuán　wèi　bǐ　sà　bǐng diàn　qǐng wèn　nín yào shén me

家　明：我 要 一 份 比 萨 饼。
jiā míng　wǒ yào yí fèn bǐ sà bǐng

店　员：您 住 在 哪 里？
diàn yuán　nín zhù zài nǎ li

家　明：我 住 在 柏 树 街 1154 号。
jiā míng　wǒ zhù zài bǎi shù jiē　hào

店　员：好，马 上 到。
diàn yuán　hǎo　mǎ shàng dào

New words

1. 喂	wèi	(exd.)	hello ①
2. 比萨饼	bǐsàbǐng	(n.)	pizza
3.(商)店	(shāng)diàn	(n.)	(business) store; shop
4. 请问	qǐngwèn	(v.)	May I ask?
5. 要	yào	(v.)	want; would like (to)
6. 份	fèn	(m.)	a set of ②
7. 住	zhù	(v.)	live; reside
8. 在	zài	(prep.)	(indicating where a person or thing is)
9. 号	hào	(n.)	number in a series ③
10. 好	hǎo	(adj.)	ok; allright
11. 马上	mǎshàng	(adv.)	right away
12. 到	dào	(v.)	arrive

Proper noun

- 柏树街 Bǎishùjiē Cypress Street

On your own: Ask and answer questions based on the following pictures.

1.

Example

① Used in receiving phone calls.

② A measure word for food here.

③ Used mostly after numericals.

一 张 光 盘
yì zhāng guāng pán

一 块 手 表
yí kuài shǒu biǎo

2.

Example

百 老 汇 大 街 2012 号
bǎi lǎo huì dà jiē hào

15 街 3325 号
shí wǔ jiē hào

Conversation practice: Substitute the alternate words to make a new dialogue.

Example

A: 请问，您要什么？
qǐng wèn nín yào shén me

B: 我要 4 份比萨饼。
wǒ yào sì fèn bǐ sà bǐng

A: 您住在哪里？
nín zhù zài nǎ li

B: 我住在 15 街 6789 号。
wǒ zhù zài shí wǔ jiē hào

A: 好，马上到。
hǎo mǎ shàng dào

1. 2 份 15 街 3325 号
liǎng fèn shí wǔ jiē hào

2. 3 份 6 街 3356 号
sān fèn liù jiē hào

3. 4 份 7 街 2899 号
sì fèn qī jiē hào

4. 1 份 柏树街 5134 号
yí fèn bǎi shù jiē hào

Class activity

Act it out: Working part-time at Pizza Hut.

Phonetics

1. Listen to the tape, and then answer the following questions.

(1) Where is the man talking?
(2) How many pieces of pizza does the woman want?
(3) Where does the woman live?

2. Read aloud the following children's song.

我是只小小鸟，
wǒ shì zhī xiǎo xiǎo niǎo

飞就飞，叫就叫，
fēi jiù fēi jiào jiù jiào

自在逍遥。
zì zài xiāo yáo

我不知有忧愁，
wǒ bù zhī yǒu yōu chóu

我不知有烦恼，
wǒ bù zhī yǒu fán nǎo

只是爱欢笑。
zhǐ shì ài huān xiào

I'm a little bird. Fly as I want, cry as I like, so free and unfettered. Not knowing worries, not knowing troubles, laugh and joy is what I want.

Learn to write

1. Structure of Chinese characters

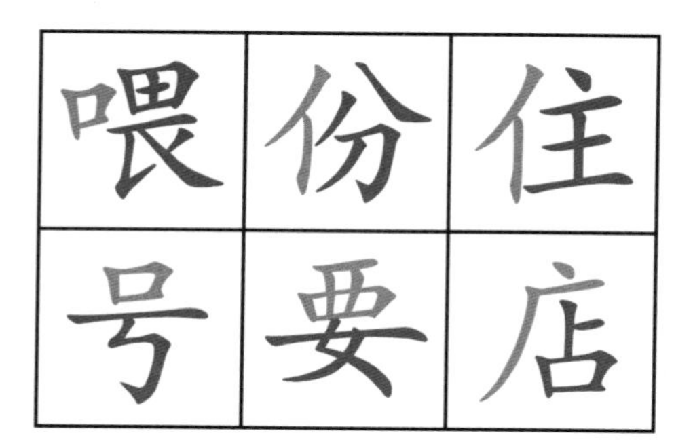

2. Examples of components

部件 bù jiàn	甲骨文 jiǎ gǔ wén	金文 jīn wén	小篆 xiǎo zhuàn	楷书 kǎi shū	组字 zǔ zì
分				分	份
主				主	住
丂				丂	号
刂				刀	到

 你家有几口人
nǐ jiā yǒu jǐ kǒu rén

In Wang Jiaming's home, David is looking at a picture above the fireplace.

大卫：你家有几口人？
dà wèi nǐ jiā yǒu jǐ kǒu rén

家明：我家有三口人。爸爸、妈妈和我。你家呢？
jiā míng wǒ jiā yǒu sān kǒu rén bà ba mā ma hé wǒ nǐ jiā ne

大卫：我家有五口人。爸爸、妈妈、哥哥、姐姐，
dà wèi wǒ jiā yǒu wǔ kǒu rén bà ba mā ma gē ge jiě jie

还有我。
hái yǒu wǒ

家明：你有没有狗？
jiā míng nǐ yǒu méi yǒu gǒu

大卫：有，我有一只大狗，还有一只小猫。
dà wèi yǒu wǒ yǒu yì zhī dà gǒu hái yǒu yì zhī xiǎo māo

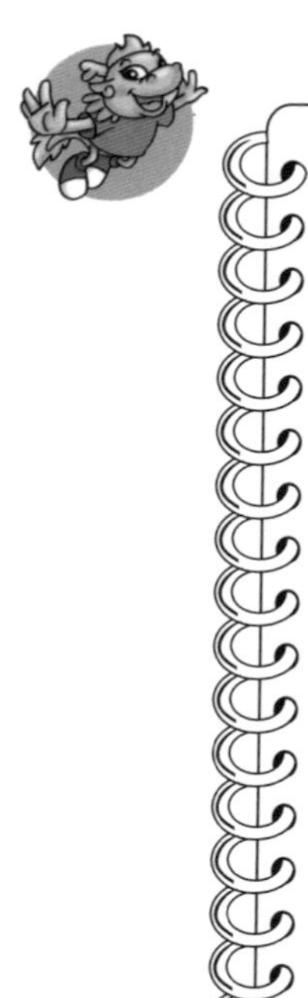

New words

1. 口	kǒu	(m.)	measure word ①
2. 人	rén	(n.)	person; people
3. 爸爸	bàba	(n.)	dad; father
4. 妈妈	māma	(n.)	mom; mother
5. 哥哥	gēge	(n.)	elder brother
6. 姐姐	jiějie	(n.)	elder sister
7. 还	hái	(adv.)	and; as well; also; too
8. 大	dà	(adj.)	big
9. 小	xiǎo	(adj.)	small; little
10. 猫	māo	(n.)	cat

On your own

1. Look at the examples and then make conversations according to the pictures.

Ann's family

A: Ann 家 有 几 口 人?
jiā yǒu jǐ kǒu rén

B: 她 家 有 四 口 人,
tā jiā yǒu sì kǒu rén

爸 爸、妈 妈、哥 哥 和 她。
bà ba mā ma gē ge hé tā

A: ________ 家 ________________?
jiā

B: 他 家 有 ________________,
tā jiā yǒu

还 有 ________________。
hái yǒu

Mike's family

① A measure word for the number of family members.

2. Big or small?

A: 这 只 狗 大 吗?
zhè zhī gǒu dà ma

B: 这 只 狗 很 大。
zhè zhī gǒu hěn dà

A: 这 只 猫 大 吗?
zhè zhī māo dà ma

B: 这 只 猫 不 大，它 很 小。
zhè zhī māo bú dà tā hěn xiǎo

A: 这 只 狗 大 吗?
zhè zhī gǒu dà ma

B: 这 只 狗 不 ______，它 很 ______。
zhè zhī gǒu bú tā hěn

A: 这 只 猫 大 吗?
zhè zhī māo dà ma

B: 这 只 猫 很 ______。
zhè zhī māo hěn

Class activity

Interview your classmates to find out how many people there are in their family.

Phonetics

1. Listen to the tape, and then answer the following questions.

(1) How many brothers does Tom have?
(2) Does Tom have any sisters?
(3) How many people are there in the girl's family?
(4) How many cats and dogs does the girl have?

2. Read aloud the following riddle and make a guess.

高 山 不 见 土，
gāo shān bú jiàn tǔ

平 地 不 见 田。
píng dì bú jiàn tián

似 海 没 有 水，
sì hǎi méi yǒu shuǐ

世 界 在 眼 前。
shì jiè zài yǎn qián

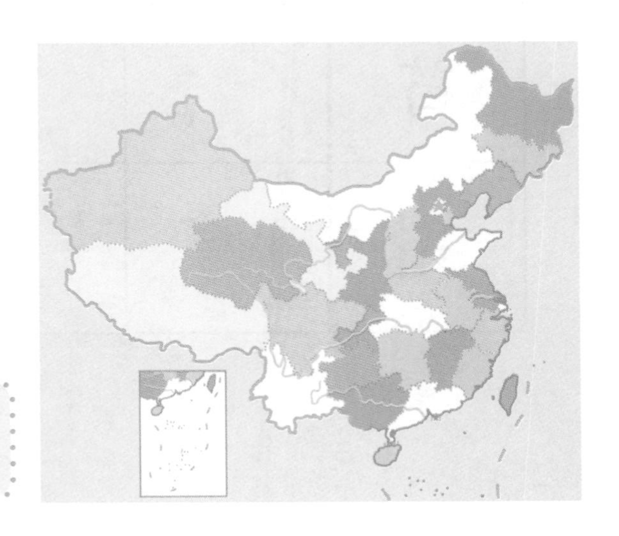

No soil on the mountain, no fields on the plain.
Like seas without water, but the world can be seen.

Learn to write

1. Structure of Chinese characters

口	人	大	小	还
妈	姐	猫	哥	爸

2. Examples of components

部件 bù jiàn	甲骨文 jiǎ gǔ wén	金文 jīn wén	小篆 xiǎo zhuàn	楷书 kǎi shū	组字 zǔ zì
父				父	爸
巴				巴	爸
可				可	哥
苗				苗	猫
辶				辵	这

18 我爸爸是医生

wǒ bà ba shì yī shēng

Mary is introducing her family.

我家有五口人，爸爸、妈妈、弟弟、妹妹和我。我们住在温哥华。我爸爸是医生。我还有爷爷和奶奶，他们不住在温哥华，他们住在芝加哥。我还有一只大狗，它叫大黄，它很喜欢我的邻居，可是我的邻居不喜欢它。

Wǒ jiā yǒu wǔ kǒu rén, bàba、māma、dìdi、mèimei hé wǒ. Wǒmen zhù zài Wēngēhuá. Wǒ bàba shì yīshēng. Wǒ hái yǒu yéye hé nǎinai, tāmen bú zhù zài Wēngēhuá, tāmén zhù zài Zhījiāgē. Wǒ hái yǒu yì zhī dà gǒu, tā jiào Dàhuáng, tā hěn xǐhuan wǒ de línjū, kěshì wǒ de línjū bù xǐhuan tā.

New words

1. 弟弟	dìdi	(n.)	younger brother
2. 妹妹	mèimei	(n.)	younger sister
3. 医生	yīshēng	(n.)	doctor
4. 爷爷	yéye	(n.)	(paternal) grandfather
5. 奶奶	nǎinai	(n.)	(paternal) grandmother
6. 喜欢	xǐhuan	(v.)	like
7. 邻居	línjū	(n.)	neighbor
8. 可是	kěshì	(conj.)	but; however

Proper nouns

- 温哥华 Wēngēhuá Vancouver
- 芝加哥 Zhījiāgē Chicago

On your own: Make sentences based on the following pictures and words.

1. What are their professions?

玛丽的爸爸是医生。
mǎ lì de bà ba shì yīshēng

大卫的爸爸 校长
dà wèi de bà ba xiào zhǎng

Anny 的 哥哥 中学生
de gē ge zhōng xué shēng

Sam 的 哥哥 音乐老师
de gē ge yīn yuè lǎo shī

2. What are their hobbies?

Emma 喜欢 听音乐。
xǐ huan tīng yīn yuè

Linda 吃蛋糕
chī dàn gāo

Jim 打橄榄球
dǎ gǎn lǎn qiú

Sam 打篮球
dǎ lán qiú

Class activity: Tell your classmates about your family.

工程师	gōngchéngshī	engineer
工人	gōngrén	factory worker
经理	jīnglǐ	manager
秘书	mìshū	secretary
推销员	tuīxiāoyuán	sales representative
记者	jìzhě	journalist
职员	zhíyuán	clerk

Phonetics

1. Listen to the tape, and then answer the following questions.

(1) What is the boy's name?
(2) How old is the boy?
(3) How many people are there in the boy's family?
(4) Where is the boy's home?
(5) Does the boy have a cat?
(6) What's the boy's dog's name?
(7) Who does not like the dog?

2. Read aloud the follwing folk song.

世 上 只 有 妈 妈 好，
shì shang zhǐ yǒu mā ma hǎo

有 妈 的 孩 子 像 个 宝，
yǒu mā de hái zi xiàng ge bǎo

投 进 妈 妈 的 怀 抱，
tóu jìn mā ma de huái bào

幸 福 有 多 少。
xìng fú yǒu duō shao

Only mum is the dearest in the world. With a mum, the child is dearly loved. Resting in her arms, he's so happy and blessed.

Can you sing it?

Learn to write

1. Structure of Chinese characters

妹	奶	邻	弟	爷
喜	可	医	居	

2. Examples of components

部件 bù jiàn	甲骨文 jiǎ gǔ wén	金文 jīn wén	小篆 xiǎo zhuàn	楷书 kǎi shū	组字 zǔ zì
令				令	邻
乃				乃	奶
卩				卩	爷
尸				尸	居
勹				勹	包

UNIT SUMMARY

FUNCTIONAL USAGE

1. Inquring about and offering age information

你 多 大?
nǐ duō dà

我 十 五 岁。
wǒ shí wǔ suì

2. Introducing oneself

我 姓 本 田,
wǒ xìng běn tián

我 叫 本 田 和 美。
wǒ jiào běn tián hé měi

3. Explaining where you come from

我 从 日 本 来。
wǒ cóng rì běn lái

4. Expressing welcome

欢 迎 你 来 我 家 玩!
huān yíng nǐ lái wǒ jiā wán

5. Ordering food on telephone

我 要 一 份 比 萨 饼。
wǒ yào yí fèn bǐ sà bǐng

6. Offering one's address

我 住 在 柏 树 街 1154 号。
wǒ zhù zài bǎi shù jiē hào

7. Inquiring about the number of people in your family

你 家 有 几 口 人?
nǐ jiā yǒu jǐ kǒu rén

我 家 有 三 口 人。
wǒ jiā yǒu sān kǒu rén

8. Stating one's profession

我 爸 爸 是 医 生。
wǒ bà ba shì yī shēng

GRAMMAR FOCUS

Sentence pattern	*Example*
1. 你 学 不 学 开 车? nǐ xué bu xué kāi chē	
2. 它 几 岁? tā jǐ suì 它 两 岁。 tā liǎng suì	
3. 从……来 cóng lái	我 从 日 本 来。 wǒ cóng rì běn lái
4. ……要…… yào	我 要 一 份 比 萨 饼。 wǒ yào yí fèn bǐ sà bǐng
5. ……有……，还 有…… yǒu hái yǒu	我 有 一 只 大 狗，还 有 一 只 小 猫。 wǒ yǒu yì zhī dà gǒu hái yǒu yì zhī xiǎo māo

Unit Four

Four Seasons of the Year

Look and Say

chūn
xià
qiū
dōng
Chūntiān zài nǎli?

19 现在几点

xiàn zài jǐ diǎn

Look and Say: What time is it now?

7:00

8:05

12:15

12:30

New words

1. 现在	xiànzài	(n.)	now
2. 点（钟）	diǎn(zhōng)	(n.)	o'clock
3. 半	bàn	(num.)	half
4. 事	shì	(n.)	matter; affair; thing; business
5. 去	qù	(v.)	go
6. 起床	qǐchuáng	(v.)	get up
7. 吧	ba	(pt.)	particle word ①

① Indicating a suggestion, a request or a mild command.

Today is Sunday. Wang Jiaming has an appointment with David, but he wakes up late.

家 明：妈 妈，现 在 几 点？
jiā míng mā ma xiàn zài jǐ diǎn

妈 妈：现 在 九 点 半。你 今 天 有 事 吗？
mā ma xiàn zài jiǔ diǎn bàn nǐ jīn tiān yǒu shì ma

家 明：我 去 大 卫 家。
jiā míng wǒ qù dà wèi jiā

妈 妈：你 几 点 去？
mā ma nǐ jǐ diǎn qù

家 明：我 十 点 去。
jiā míng wǒ shí diǎn qù

妈 妈：起 床 吧！
mā ma qǐ chuáng ba

On your own: Ask and answer questions based on the following pictures.

A：现 在 几 点?
xiàn zài jǐ diǎn

B：现 在 十 点 半。
xiàn zài shí diǎn bàn

A：现 在________?
xiàn zài

B：现 在________。
xiàn zài

A：现 在 5 点 10 分，对 吗?
xiàn zài wǔ diǎn shí fēn duì ma

B：对，________。
duì

A：现 在 7 点 半，对 吗?
xiàn zài qī diǎn bàn duì ma

B：不 对，________。
bú duì

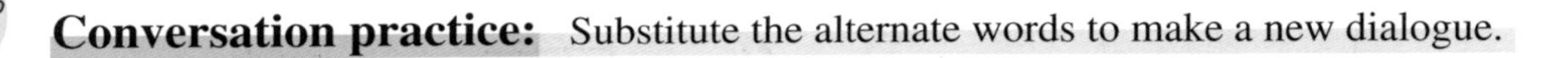

Conversation practice: Substitute the alternate words to make a new dialogue.

1.

A：请 问，现 在 几 点?
qǐngwèn xiàn zài jǐ diǎn

B：十 点 十 五 分。
shí diǎn shí wǔ fēn

A：谢 谢 您!
xiè xie nín

B：不 客 气!
bú kè qi

1. 七 点 二 十
qī diǎn èr shí

2. 八 点 半
bā diǎn bàn

3. 十 二 点
shí èr diǎn

2.

A：你 今 天 有 事 吗?
nǐ jīn tiān yǒu shì ma

B：我 今 天 没 有 事。
wǒ jīn tiān méi yǒu shì

你 有 事 吗?
nǐ yǒu shì ma

A：我 十 点 去 大 卫 家。
wǒ shí diǎn qù dà wèi jiā

1. 十 二 点 比 萨 饼 店
shí èr diǎn bǐ sà bǐng diàn

2. 三 点 半 打 网 球
sān diǎn bàn dǎ wǎng qiú

3. 七 点 半 听 音 乐
qī diǎn bàn tīng yīn yuè

Class activity: Make a clock.

With a partner, use a piece of cardboard and a pin to make a clock with movable hands. Afterwards, take turns changing the positions of the clock hands and stating the time.

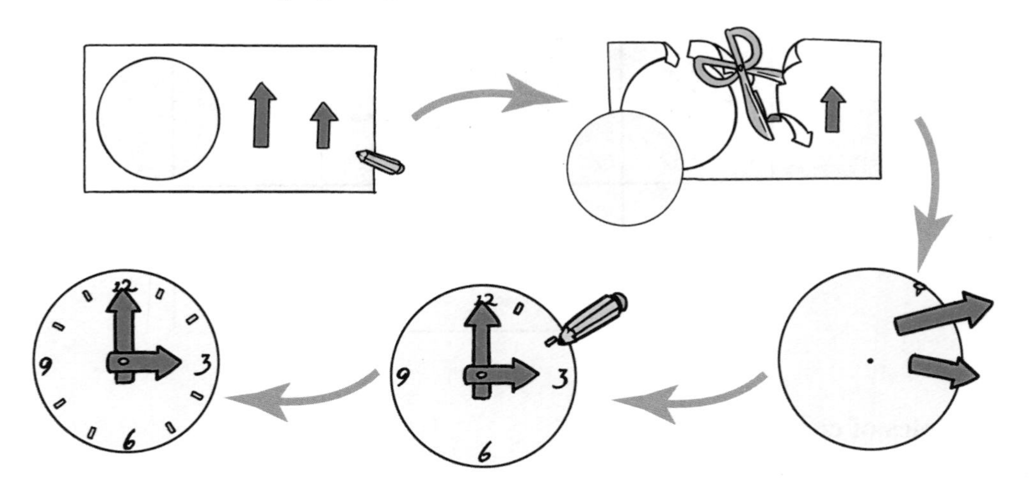

Phonetics

1. Listen to the tape, and then answer the following questions.

(1) What is the mother going to do today?

(2) What time is it when the mother and her daughter have the conversation?

(3) What is the girl going to do today?

2. Read the following Chinese ancient poem.

春 眠 不 觉 晓，
chūn mián bù jué xiǎo

处 处 闻 啼 鸟。
chù chù wén tí niǎo

夜 来 风 雨 声，
yè lái fēng yǔ shēng

花 落 知 多 少！
huā luò zhī duō shǎo

It's after dawn when I awoke this morning in spring. Then everywhere around me I heard birds all sing. I now recall the sound of big storm late at night. How many flowers would have been blown to ground in sight?

Learn to write

1. Structure of Chinese characters

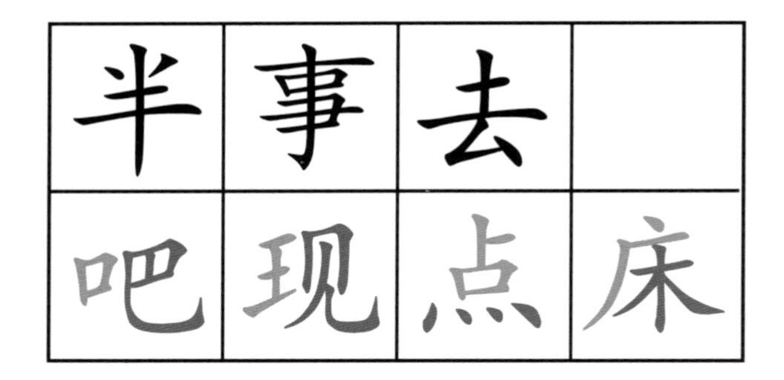

2. Examples of components

部件 bù jiàn	甲骨文 jiǎ gǔ wén	金文 jīn wén	小篆 xiǎo zhuàn	楷书 kǎi shū	组字 zǔ zì
广		广	广	广	床
占	占		占	占	点
豕	豕	豕	豕	豕	家

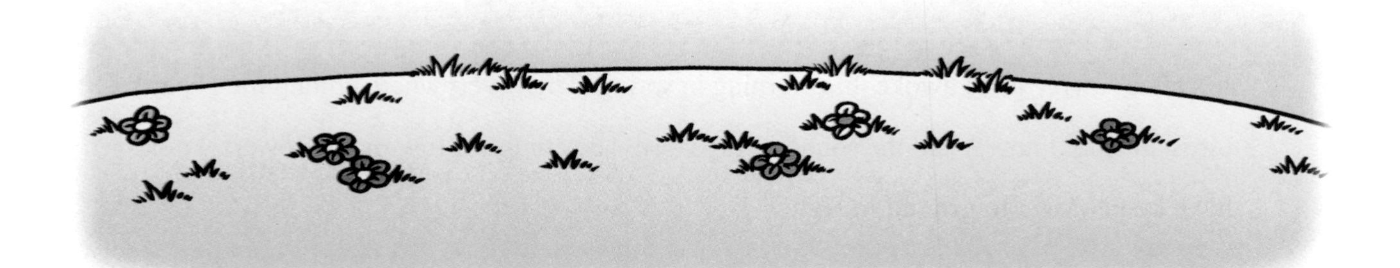

你每天几点起床

nǐ měi tiān jǐ diǎn qǐ chuáng

Look and Say

早上 **7:05** 起床

8:30 上学

中午 **12:00** 吃饭

下午 **3:15** 放学

晚上 **10:20** 睡觉

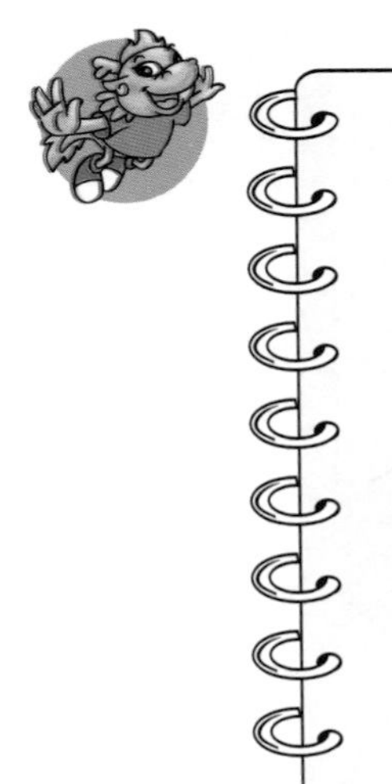

New words

1. 每天	měi tiān		every day
2. 早上	zǎoshang	(n.)	morning
3. 刻（钟）	kè (zhōng)	(n.)	a quarter of an hour
4. 晚上	wǎnshang	(n.)	night; evening
5. 时候	shíhou	(n.)	time; moment
6. 睡觉	shuìjiào	(v.)	go to bed; sleep

Wang Jiaming is at David's. They are talking about their work-and-rest schedules.

家明：大卫，你每天早上几点起床？
jiā míng dà wèi nǐ měi tiān zǎo shang jǐ diǎn qǐ chuáng

大卫：我每天七点一刻起床。
dà wèi wǒ měi tiān qī diǎn yí kè qǐ chuáng

家明：晚上呢，晚上你什么时候睡觉？
jiā míng wǎn shang ne wǎn shang nǐ shén me shí hou shuì jiào

大卫：我十点半睡觉。你呢？
dà wèi wǒ shí diǎn bàn shuì jiào nǐ ne

家明：我早上七点起床，晚上十一点睡觉。
jiā míng wǒ zǎo shang qī diǎn qǐ chuáng wǎn shang shí yī diǎn shuì jiào

Read aloud

早上
zǎoshang

上午
shàng wǔ

中午
zhōng wǔ

下午
xià wǔ

晚上
wǎnshang

On your own: Ask and answer questions based on the given words.

A：你几点起床？
nǐ jǐ diǎn qǐchuáng

B：我六点起床。
wǒ liù diǎn qǐchuáng

1. 上课[①] shàngkè	九点 jiǔ diǎn	3. 回家[③] huí jiā	四点 sì diǎn
2. 下课[②] xià kè	三点 sān diǎn	4. 睡觉 shuì jiào	十一点 shí yī diǎn

Class activity: Interview your classmates about their daily routine.

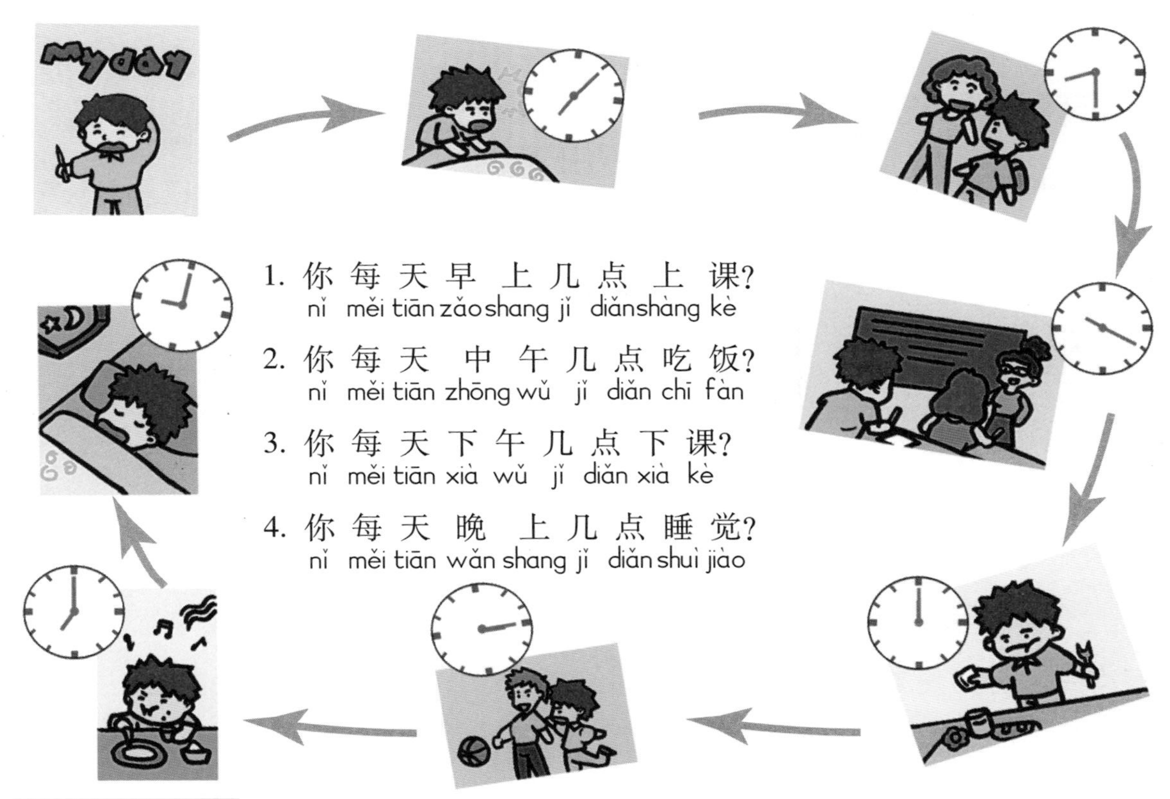

1. 你每天早上几点上课？
nǐ měi tiān zǎoshang jǐ diǎn shàng kè

2. 你每天中午几点吃饭？
nǐ měi tiān zhōng wǔ jǐ diǎn chī fàn

3. 你每天下午几点下课？
nǐ měi tiān xià wǔ jǐ diǎn xià kè

4. 你每天晚上几点睡觉？
nǐ měi tiān wǎn shang jǐ diǎn shuì jiào

---

① Go to school.
② Finish classes.
③ Go home.

Phonetics

1. Listen to the tape, and then answer the following questions.

(1) When does David play basketball every day?

(2) When does David study Chinese every day?

2. Read the following Chinese riddle and make a guess.

会 走 没 有 腿，
huì zǒu méi yǒu tuǐ

会 叫 没 有 嘴。
huì jiào méi yǒu zuǐ

它 会 告 诉 我 们，
tā huì gào su wǒ men

什 么 时 候 起，
shén me shí hou qǐ

什 么 时 候 睡。
shén me shí hou shuì

Without legs or mouth, but it can both walk and talk. It can tell us when to awake and when to sleep.

Learn to write

1. Structure of Chinese characters

上			
刻	时	候	睡
每	早	觉	

2. Examples of components

部件 bù jiàn	甲骨文 jiǎ gǔ wén	金文 jīn wén	小篆 xiǎo zhuàn	楷书 kǎi shū	组字 zǔ zì
亥				亥	刻
目				目	睡
母				母	每
𠂉				𠂉	每

昨天、今天、明天

zuó tiān　jīn tiān　míng tiān

Look and Say

New words

1. 昨天	zuótiān	(n.)	yesterday
2. 明天	míngtiān	(n.)	tomorrow
3. 月	yuè	(n.)	month
4. 号	hào	(n.)	date ③
5. 节	jié	(n.)	holiday; festival
6. 哪	nǎ	(pron.)	which
7. 天	tiān	(n.)	day
8. 明年	míngnián	(n.)	next year

Proper nouns

- 感恩节 Gǎn'ēn Jié Thanksgiving Day
- 中国 Zhōngguó China
- 春节 Chūn Jié The Spring Festival (Chinese Lunar New Year)

---

①② Chinese lunar calendar.

③ Used mostly after numericals, here for date of month.

Wang Jiaming is asking Mary today's date when David joins them.

家 明：今 天 几 月 几 号？
jiā míng jīn tiān jǐ yuè jǐ hào

玛 丽：十 一 月 二 十 三 号。
mǎ lì shí yī yuè èr shí sān hào

家 明：感 恩 节 是 哪 一 天？
jiā míng gǎn ēn jié shì nǎ yì tiān

玛 丽：明 天。
mǎ lì míng tiān

大 卫：中 国 的 春 节 是 哪 一 天？
dà wèi zhōng guó de chūn jié shì nǎ yì tiān

家 明：明 年 一 月 十 六 日 是 春 节。
jiā míng míng nián yī yuè shí liù rì shì chūn jié

Time expressions

昨 天 (yesterday)
zuó tiān

今 天 (today)
jīn tiān

明 天 (tomorrow)
míng tiān

去 年 (last year)
qù nián

今 年 (this year)
jīn nián

明 年 (next year)
míng nián

Do you know how many days are there in each month?

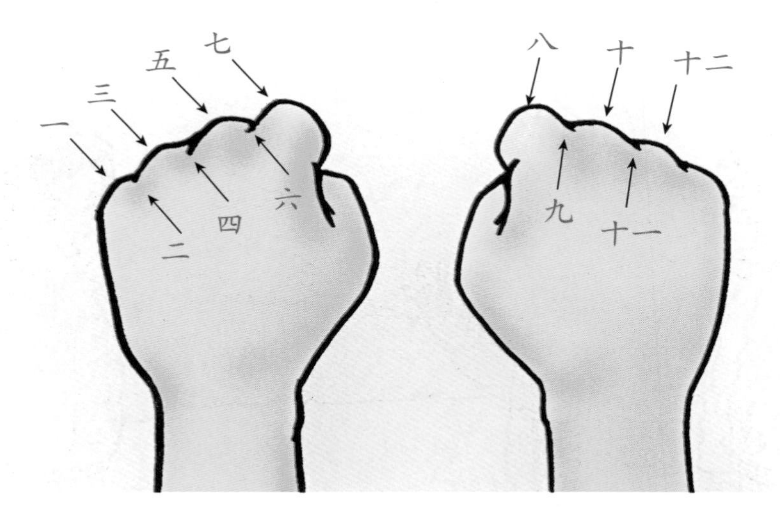

一 月 大[①] yī yuè dà	二 月 小 èr yuèxiǎo	三 月 大 sān yuè dà	四 月 小 sì yuèxiǎo
五 月 大 wǔ yuè dà	六 月 小 liù yuèxiǎo	七 月 大 qī yuè dà	八 月 大 bā yuè dà
九 月 小 jiǔ yuèxiǎo	十 月 大 shí yuè dà	十 一 月 小 shí yī yuèxiǎo	十 二 月 大 shí èr yuè dà

① The "big month" refers to the solar month of 31 days, and the "small month" refers to the solar month of 30 days. Feburary is an exception. There are 29 days in Feburary once every four years, and in the remaining three years, it has only 28 days.

Interview a partner

1. 今 天 几 月 几 号?
   jīn tiān jǐ yuè jǐ hào
2. 昨 天 几 月 几 号?
   zuó tiān jǐ yuè jǐ hào
3. 明 天 几 月 几 号?
   míngtiān jǐ yuè jǐ hào

Conversation practice: Substitute the alternate words to make a new dialogue.

A：请 问，今 天 几 月 几 号?
qǐng wèn jīn tiān jǐ yuè jǐ hào

B：今 天 十 一 月 二 十 四 号。
jīn tiān shí yī yuè èr shí sì hào

A：啊，今 天 是 感 恩 节。谢 谢 您!
a jīn tiān shì gǎn ēn jié xiè xiè nín

B：不 客 气。
bú kè qi

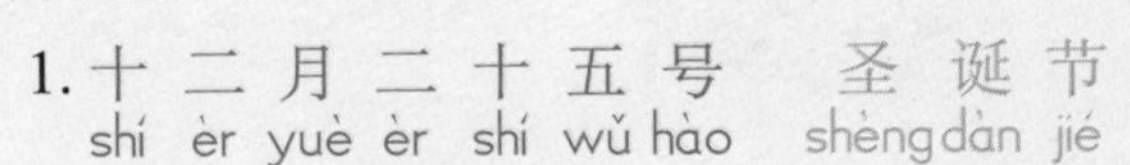

1. 十 二 月 二 十 五 号 圣 诞 节
   shí èr yuè èr shí wǔ hào shèngdàn jié
2. 一 月 十 六 号 春 节
   yī yuè shí liù hào chūn jié

Class activity: Which is your favorite holiday?

Western Holidays

Shèngdàn Jié

Gǎn'ēn Jié

Fùhuó Jié

Qíngrén Jié

Chinese Holidays

Chūn Jié

Yuánxiāo Jié

Duānwǔ Jié

Zhōngqiū Jié

Phonetics

1. Listen to the tape, and then answer the following questions.

(1) What's the date of today?

(2) When is the father's birthday?

2. Read the following ancient Chinese poem.

白 日 依 山 尽，
bái rì yī shān jìn

黄 河 入 海 流，
huáng hé rù hǎi liú

欲 穷 千 里 目，
yù qióng qiān lǐ mù

更 上 一 层 楼。
gèng shàng yì céng lóu

Way down behind the hills the sun is going.
Into the sea the Yellow River's flowing.
Wanting to see as far as my eyes could, climb
up still one more flight of stairs I should.

Learn to write

1. Structure of Chinese characters

月	年	昨	国
节	感	恩	春

2. Examples of components

部件 bù jiàn	甲骨文 jiǎ gǔ wén	金文 jīn wén	小篆 xiǎo zhuàn	楷书 kǎi shū	组字 zǔ zì
艹				草	节
⺪				⺪	是
白				白	的

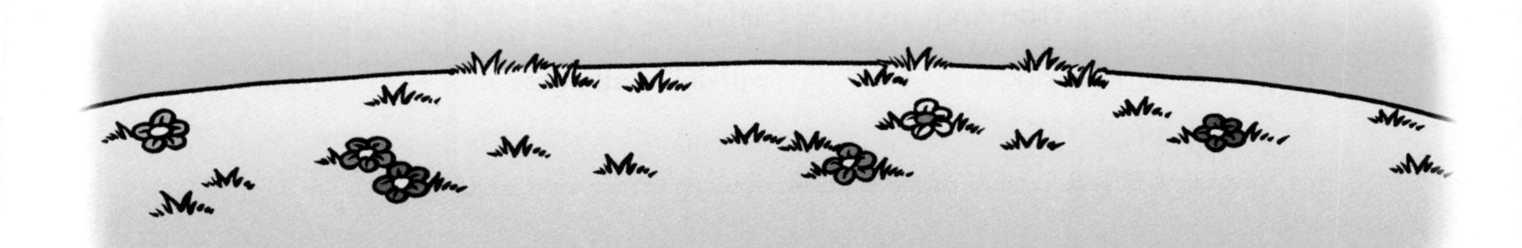

星期六你干什么
xīng qī liù nǐ gàn shén me

Look and Say

Jack's timetable

星期一

上学
shàng xué

星期二

打球
dǎ qiú

星期三

学汉语
xué hàn yǔ

星期四

听音乐
tīng yīn yuè

星期五

去朋友家
qù péng you jiā

星期六

看电影
kàn diànyǐng

星期日

上网
shàng wǎng

New words

1. 星期	xīngqī	(n.)	day of the week [①]
2. 打算	dǎsuàn	(n.;v.)	plan (to); be going to
3. 干	gàn	(v.)	do
4. 看	kàn	(v.)	see; look at; watch
5. 电影	diànyǐng	(n.)	movie
6. 行	xíng	(v.)	will do; be all right
7. 可以	kěyǐ	(v.;aux.)	can; may

① Used in combination with 日，一，二，三，四，五，六 to denote day of the week.

Mary wants to go to see a movie with Wang Jiaming, David and Jack.

玛 丽：家 明，星 期 六 你 打 算 干 什 么？
mǎ lì jiā míng xīng qī liù nǐ dǎ suàn gàn shén me

家 明：我 打 算 跟 大 卫、杰 克 一 起 看 电 影。
jiā míng wǒ dǎ suàn gēn dà wèi jié kè yì qǐ kàn diàn yǐng

你 打 算 干 什 么？
nǐ dǎ suàn gàn shén me

玛 丽：我 跟 你 们 一 起 去 看 电 影，行 吗？
mǎ lì wǒ gēn nǐ men yì qǐ qù kàn diàn yǐng xíng ma

家 明：当 然 可 以。
jiā míng dāng rán kě yǐ

Read and match

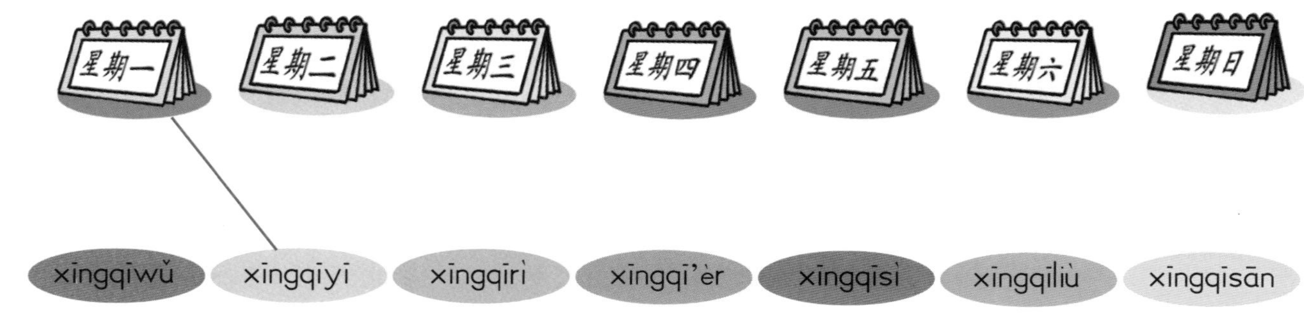

Conversation practice: Substitute the alternate words to make a new dialogue.

A：杰 克，星 期 六 你 打 算 干 什 么？
jié kè xīng qī liù nǐ dǎ suàn gàn shén me

B：我 跟 朋 友 们 一 起 去 打 橄 榄 球，
wǒ gēn péng you men yì qǐ qù dǎ gǎn lǎn qiú

你 呢？ 打 算 干 什 么？
nǐ ne dǎ suàn gàn shén me

A：我 跟 你 们 一 起 去 打 橄 榄 球，可
wǒ gēn nǐ men yì qǐ qù dǎ gǎn lǎn qiú kě

以 吗？
yǐ ma

B：当 然 可 以。（对 不 起①，不 行）
dāngrán kě yǐ duì bu qǐ bù xíng

1. 星 期 日 xīng qī rì	Steven、Bill	学 开 车 xué kāi chē
2. 今 天 jīn tiān	Tom、Fred	打 网 球 dǎ wǎngqiú
3. 明 天 míngtiān	Jane、Betty	看 电 影 kàn diànyǐng

Interview a partner

1. 一 个 星 期 有 几 天？
yí ge xīng qī yǒu jǐ tiān

2. 今 天 星 期 几？
jīn tiān xīng qī jǐ

3. 这 个 星 期 六、星 期 日 你 打 算 干 什 么？
zhè ge xīng qī liù xīng qī rì nǐ dǎ suan gàn shén me

① I'm sorry.

Class activity: Make up your own Chinese movie poster.

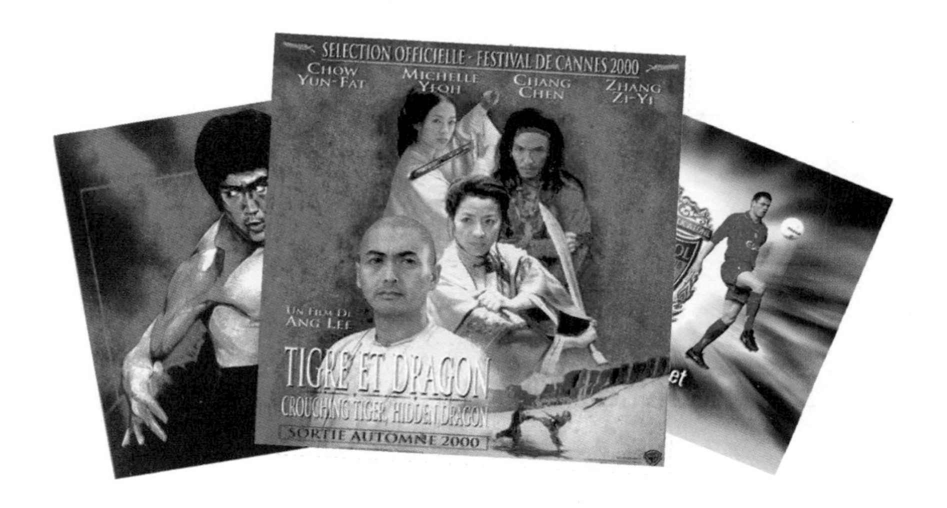

Phonetics

1. Listen to the tape, and then answer the following questions.

(1) What is Mary going to do this Sunday?

(2) Whom is Mary going with?

(3) What is the boy going to do this Sunday?

2. Read aloud the following children's song.

我是小金鱼，住在池塘里，
wǒ shì xiǎo jīn yú zhù zài chí táng lǐ

游过来，游过去，总是不如意。
yóu guò lái yóu guò qù zǒng shì bù rú yì

努力游，努力游，游过了小河，
nǔ lì yóu nǔ lì yóu yóu guò le xiǎo hé

一天又一天，来到大海里。
yì tiān yòu yì tiān lái dào dà hǎi lǐ

I'm a little goldfish living in a pond. Swimming to and fro, but I couldn't have fun. Struggling and struggling, finally I left the creek behind. Day after day, eventually I reached the ocean.

Learn to write

1. Structure of Chinese characters

干	电	看	算	
期	跟	影	行	以

2. Examples of components

部件 bù jiàn	甲骨文 jiǎ gǔ wén	金文 jīn wén	小篆 xiǎo zhuàn	楷书 kǎi shū	组字 zǔ zì
其				其	期
⻊				足	跟
景				景	影
龵				龵	看

23 今天天气怎么样

jīn tiān tiān qì zěn me yàng

Look and Say

New words

1. 天气	tiānqì	(n.)	weather
2. 怎么样	zěnmeyàng	(pron.)	how
3. 刮（风）	guā(fēng)	(v.)	(of wind) blow
4. 风	fēng	(n.)	wind
5. 下午	xiàwǔ	(n.)	afternoon
6. 可能	kěnéng	(aux.)	maybe; perhaps
7. 下雨	xià yǔ		rain
8. 带	dài	(v.)	take/bring/carry... with sb.
9. 雨伞	yǔsǎn	(n.)	umbrella
10. 哪儿	nǎr	(pron.)	where
11. 外面	wàimian	(n.)	outside
12. 雨衣	yǔyī	(n.)	raincoat

Wang Jiaming is about to go to school and he is asking his father about today's weather.

家 明：爸 爸，今 天 天 气 怎 么 样？
jiā míng bà ba jīn tiān tiān qì zěn me yàng

爸 爸：现 在 刮 风，下 午 可 能 下 雨。
bà ba xiàn zài guā fēng xià wǔ kě néng xià yǔ

家 明：我 带 雨 伞 吧，我 的 雨 伞 在 哪 儿？
jiā míng wǒ dài yǔ sǎn ba wǒ de yǔ sǎn zài nǎr

爸 爸：外 面 风 很 大，你 带 雨 衣 吧！
bà ba wài mian fēng hěn dà nǐ dài yǔ yī ba

Read aloud

刮 风　　下 雨
guā fēng　　xià yǔ

带 雨 伞　　带 雨 衣
dài yǔ sǎn　　dài yǔ yī

一 把[①] 雨 伞　　一 件 雨 衣
yì bǎ yǔ sǎn　　yí jiàn yǔ yī

现 在 外 面 风 很 大　　现 在 外 面 雨 很 大
xiàn zài wàimian fēng hěn dà　　xiàn zài wàimian yǔ hěn dà

On your own

1. Match the pictures with the words.

下 雨、刮 风
xià yǔ guāfēng

下 雨
xià yǔ

雨 伞
yǔ sǎn

雨 衣
yǔ yī

2. Look at the example and then make conversations according to the given words.

Example

A：今 天 天 气 怎 么 样?
jīn tiān tiān qì zěn me yàng

B：今 天 可 能 下 雨。
jīn tiān kě néng xià yǔ

1. 明 天　　下 雨
míngtiān　　xià yǔ
2. 星 期 六　　刮 风
xīng qī liù　　guāfēng
3. 后 天　　下 雪
hòu tiān　　xià xuě
4. 星 期 日　　刮 风、下 雨
xīng qī rì　　guāfēng xià yǔ

①把：A measure word, used of a tool with a handle.

Class activity

1. Chart the weather this week and make a weather map. Be your own meteorologist!

星期一 xīng qī yī	星期二 xīng qī èr	星期三 xīng qī sān	星期四 xīng qī sì	星期五 xīng qī wǔ	星期六 xīng qī liù	星期日 xīng qī rì

2. Discuss your weather map with a partner.

Example

A：星期六天气怎么样?
xīng qī liù tiān qì zěn me yàng

B：星期六天气很好。你打算干什么?
xīng qī liù tiān qì hěn hǎo nǐ dǎ suàn gàn shén me

Phonetics

1. Listen to the tape, and then answer the following questions.

(1) Is it raining outside?

(2) Is the wind blowing outside?

(3) What does the boy ask the woman to take with her?

2. Read aloud the following tongue twister.

他喜欢琵琶，我喜欢吉他。
tā xǐ huan pí pá wǒ xǐ huan jí tā

他说琵琶好，我说吉他好。
tā shuō pí pá hǎo wǒ shuō jí tā hǎo

现在你来听，
xiàn zài nǐ lái tīng

是琵琶好还是吉他好。
shì pí pá hǎo hái shì jí tā hǎo

He likes *pipa* ①; I like guitars. He says *pipa* is better than guitars; I say a guitar is better than *pipa*. Now you can listen which is better, *pipa* or guitars?

---

① *Pipa*: a plucked string instrument with a fretted fingerboard.

Learn to write

1. Structure of Chinese characters

下	雨	面	伞	午
样	刮	能	外	带

2. Examples of components

部件 bù jiàn	甲骨文 jiǎ gǔ wén	金文 jīn wén	小篆 xiǎo zhuàn	楷书 kǎi shū	组字 zǔ zì
羊				羊	样
巾				巾	带
几				几	风

24 冬天冷，夏天热

dōng tiān lěng xià tiān rè

Look and Say

冬天冷，夏天热，春天常常刮风，秋天不冷也不热。

Winter is cold; summer is hot; spring is extremely windy; fall is neither cold nor hot.

冬 天
dōng tiān

夏 天
xià tiān

春 天
chūn tiān

秋 天
qiū tiān

New words

1. 新年	xīnnián	(n.)	New Year
2. 最近	zuìjìn	(n.)	recently; lately
3. 忙	máng	(adj.)	busy
4. 觉得	juéde	(v.)	think; feel
5. 秋天	qiūtiān	(n.)	fall
6. 最	zuì	(adv.)	most; least; best; to the highest or lowest degree
7. 冬天	dōngtiān	(n.)	winter
8. 冷	lěng	(adj.)	cold
9. 夏天	xiàtiān	(n.)	summer
10. 热	rè	(adj.)	hot
11. 春天	chūntiān	(n.)	spring
12. 常常	chángcháng	(adv.)	often
13. 非常	fēicháng	(adv.)	very
14. 节日	jiérì	(n.)	holiday; red-letter day

Proper noun

- 北京 Běijīng Beijing
- 小雨 Xiǎoyǔ a person's name, literally "drizzle"

Wang Jiaming has just received a letter from one of his friends in Beijing.

家明：

新年好！

最近忙不忙？你打算什么时候来北京？北京的冬天很冷，夏天很热。春天不冷，可是常常刮风。秋天非常好，不冷也不热。我觉得秋天最好。

祝你

节日快乐！

你的朋友：小雨

1月5日

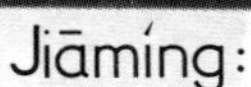

Jiāmíng:

Xīnnián hǎo!

Zuìjìn máng bu máng? Nǐ dǎsuàn shénme shíhou lái Běijīng? Běijīng de dōngtiān hěn lěng, xiàtiān hěn rè. Chūntiān bù lěng, kěshì chángcháng guā fēng. Qiūtiān fēicháng hǎo, bù lěng yě bú rè. Wǒ juéde qiūtiān zuì hǎo.

Zhù nǐ

jiérì kuàilè!

Nǐ de péngyou: Xiǎoyǔ

yī yuè wǔ rì

Read aloud

祝 你 生 日 快 乐!
zhù nǐ shēng ri kuài lè

祝 你 新 年 快 乐!
zhù nǐ xīn nián kuài lè

祝 你 节 日 快 乐!
zhù nǐ jié rì kuài lè

On your own: Make conversations according to the example and given words.

1. A：最 近 忙 不 忙?
zuì jìn máng bu máng

B：很 忙。
hěn máng

1. 非 常 忙
fēi cháng máng
2. 有 点 儿 忙
yǒu diǎnr máng
3. 不 太 忙
bú tài máng

2. A：最 近 怎 么 样?
zuì jìn zěn me yàng

B：还 好。
hái hǎo

1. 非 常 忙
fēi cháng máng
2. 还 不 错
hái bú cuò
3. 很 不 好
hěn bù hǎo

Interview a partner

1. 你 觉 得 北 京 的 天 气 怎 么 样?
nǐ jué de běi jīng de tiān qì zěn me yàng
2. 你 们 这 里 的 天 气 好 不 好?
nǐ men zhè lǐ de tiān qì hǎo bu hǎo
3. 这 里 夏 天 热 不 热? 冬 天 冷 不 冷?
zhè lǐ xià tiān rè bu rè dōng tiān lěng bu lěng
4. 你 觉 得 哪 个 季 节 最 好?
nǐ jué de nǎ ge jì jié zuì hǎo

Writing

Use Chinese to write a letter to a friend living in another city. Describe the weather in your city and don't forget to ask when they are coming for a visit at the end of the letter.

Phonetics

1. Listen to the tape, and then answer the following questions.

(1) Where is the woman?

(2) What is the boy going to do?

(3) Is it in spring or in summer when they have this telephone conversation?

(4) Has Ms. Wang been busy these days?

(5) Does Ms. Wang invite David to come to Beijing?

2. Read aloud the following children's song.

春 天 在 哪 里 呀，春 天 在 哪 里？
chūn tiān zài nǎ li ya chūn tiān zài nǎ li
春 天 在 那 青 翠 的 山 林 里，
chūn tiān zài nà qīng cuì de shān lín lǐ
这 里 有 红 花 呀，这 里 有 绿 草，
zhè lǐ yǒu hóng huā ya zhè lǐ yǒu lǜ cǎo
还 有 那 会 唱 歌 的 小 黄 鹂。
hái yǒu nà huì chàng gē de xiǎo huáng lí

Where is spring? Where is spring? Spring lies in the green woods, with red flowers and green grass, and the singing little orioles.

Sing a song

嘀哩嘀哩
dī li dī li
望安 词
潘振声 曲
春天在哪里呀，春天在哪里？
春天在那青翠的山林里，
这里有红花呀，这里有绿草，
还有那会唱歌的小黄鹂。
di li li di li di li li, di li li di li li,
di li li di li di li li, di li li di li li!
春天在青翠的山林里，
还有那会唱歌的小黄鹂。

Learn to write

1. Structure of Chinese characters

新	忙	秋	冷	非
冬	夏	最	热	常

2. Examples of components

部件 bù jiàn	甲骨文 jiǎ gǔ wén	金文 jīn wén	小篆 xiǎo zhuàn	楷书 kǎi shū	组字 zǔ zì
斤				斤	新 近
亡				亡	忙
夂				夂	冬 夏
冫				冫	冷

UNIT SUMMARY

FUNCTIONAL USAGE

1. Inquiring about and giving the time

现 在 几 点? 现 在 九 点 半。
xiàn zài jǐ diǎn xiàn zài jiǔ diǎn bàn

2. Explaining one's schedule

我 每 天 七 点 一 刻 起 床。
wǒ měi tiān qī diǎn yí kè qǐ chuáng

3. Inquiring about and giving the date

今 天 几 月 几 号?
jīn tiān jǐ yuè jǐ hào

今 天 十 一 月 二 十 三 号。
jīn tiān shí yī yuè èr shí sān hào

4. Inquring about and explaining one's plans

星 期 六 你 打 算 干 什 么?
xīng qī liù nǐ dǎ suàn gàn shén me

我 打 算 跟 大 卫、杰 克 一 起 看 电 影。
wǒ dǎ suàn gēn dà wèi jié kè yì qǐ kàn diàn yǐng

5. Inquiring about and telling the weather

今 天 天 气 怎 么 样?
jīn tiān tiān qì zěn me yàng

现 在 刮 风, 下 午 可 能 下 雨。
xiàn zài guā fēng xià wǔ kě néng xià yǔ

6. Expressing one's opinions

我 觉 得 北 京 的 秋 天 最 好。
wǒ jué de běi jīng de qiū tiān zuì hǎo

7. Explaining the climate

冬 天 很 冷, 夏 天 很 热,
dōng tiān hěn lěng xià tiān hěn rè

秋 天 不 冷 也 不 热。
qiū tiān bù lěng yě bú rè

GRAMMAR FOCUS

Sentence pattern	Example
1. 现 在 九 点 半。 xiàn zài jiǔ diǎn bàn	
2. 我 每 天 七 点 一 刻 起 床。 wǒ měi tiān qī diǎn yí kè qǐ chuáng	
3. 今 天 十 一 月 二 十 三 号。 jīn tiān shí yī yuè èr shí sān hào	
4. ……跟……一 起 gēn yì qǐ	我 跟 你 们 一 起 去 看 电 影。 wǒ gēn nǐ men yì qǐ qù kàn diàn yǐng
5. ……打 算…… dǎ suàn	我 打 算 跟 大 卫 一 起 看 电 影。 wǒ dǎ suan gēn dà wèi yì qǐ kàn diàn yǐng
6. ……怎 么 样 zěn me yàng	今 天 天 气 怎 么 样? jīn tiān tiān qì zěn me yàng
7. ……觉 得…… jué de	我 觉 得 北 京 的 秋 天 最 好。 wǒ jué de běi jīng de qiū tiān zuì hǎo

Unit Five

Food and Clothing

Look and Say

Wǒ yào èrshí ge jiǎozi.
Yígòng duōshao qián?
Chuān zhè jiàn háishi chuān nà jiàn?

我要二十个饺子

wǒ yào èr shí ge jiǎo zi

Look and Say

New words

1. 先生	xiānsheng	(n.)	mister; sir; gentleman
2. (一)点(儿)	(yì)diǎn(r)	(m.)	a little; a bit; some (here something)
3. 饺子	jiǎozi	(n.)	dumpling
4. 个	gè	(m.)	measure word ①
5. 喝	hē	(v.)	drink
6. 饮料	yǐnliào	(n.)	beverage
7. 碗	wǎn	(m.)	bowl
8. 鸡蛋	jīdàn	(n.)	egg
9. 汤	tāng	(n.)	soup

① Usually used before a noun having no particular classifier.

Jack is eating dinner at a Chinese restaurant.

服务员：先生，您吃点儿什么？
fú wù yuán xiān sheng nín chī diǎnr shén me

杰　克：有饺子吗？
jié kè yǒu jiǎo zi ma

服务员：有，要多少？
fú wù yuán yǒu yào duō shao

杰　克：二十个饺子。
jié kè èr shí ge jiǎo zi

服务员：好。您喝什么饮料？
fú wù yuán hǎo nín hē shén me yǐn liào

杰　克：我不要饮料，要一碗鸡蛋汤。
jié kè wǒ bú yào yǐn liào yào yì wǎn jī dàn tāng

服务员：好。
fú wù yuán hǎo

Read and match

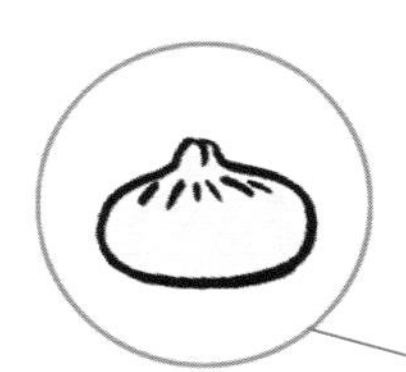

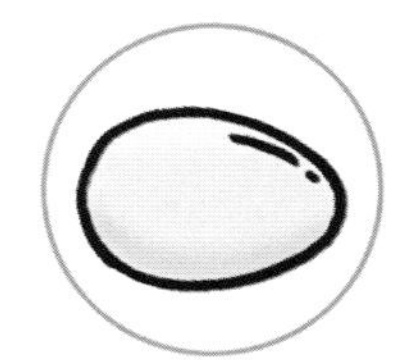

一个饺子 yí ge jiǎo zi	一个鸡蛋 yí ge jī dàn	一个包子 yí ge bāo zi	一碗汤 yì wǎn tāng	一份蛋炒饭 yí fèn dànchǎofàn

Conversation practice: Substitute the alternate words to make a new dialogue.

A：您好！您吃点儿什么？
nín hǎo nín chī diǎnr shén me

B：二十个饺子。
èr shí ge jiǎo zi

A：您喝点儿什么？
nín hē diǎnr shén me

B：我不要饮料，要一碗汤。
wǒ bú yào yǐn liào yào yì wǎn tāng

1. 六个包子
liù ge bāo zi

2. 十个包子
shí ge bāo zi

3. 一份蛋炒饭
yí fèn dàn chǎo fàn

Class activity

You have $15 to spend. What would you like to eat?

饺子	jiǎozi	Dumplings	$3
包子	bāozi	Steamed stuffed bun	$3
蛋炒饭	dànchǎofàn	Fried rice with eggs	$5
鸡蛋汤	jīdàntāng	Egg soup	$2
酸甜肉	suāntiánròu	Sweet and sour meat	$10

Phonetics

1. Listen to the tape, and then answer the following questions.

(1) What would he like to eat?

(2) How much does he want?

(3) Does he want anything to drink?

2. Read aloud the following Chinese ancient poem.

锄 禾 日 当 午，
chú hé rì dāng wǔ

汗 滴 禾 下 土。
hàn dī hé xià tǔ

谁 知 盘 中 餐，
shuí zhī pán zhōng cān

粒 粒 皆 辛 苦。
lì lì jiē xīn kǔ

At noon they hoe up weeds.
Their sweat drips on the soil.
Who knows the rice that feeds
is the fruit of hard toil!

Learn to write

1. Structure of Chinese characters

子	个	先	饺
喝	饮	料	鸡
汤	碗		

2. Examples of components

部件 bù jiàn	甲骨文 jiǎ gǔ wén	金文 jīn wén	小篆 xiǎo zhuàn	楷书 kǎi shū	组字 zǔ zì
饣				食	饺 饮
石				石	碗
鸟				鸟(鳥)	鸡
𠃓				𠃓(昜)	汤

你们家买不买年货
nǐ men jiā mǎi bu mǎi nián huò

Look and Say

年货
nián huò

压岁钱
yā suì qián

礼物
lǐ wù

New words

1. 热闹	rènao	(adj.)	busy; bustling
2. 为什么	wèishénme		why
3. 因为	yīnwèi	(conj.)	because
4. 后天	hòutiān	(n.)	the day after tomorrow
5. 买	mǎi	(v.)	buy
6. 年货	niánhuò	(n.)	special purchases for the Spring Festival
7. 过年	guònián	(v.)	celebrate the New Year or the Spring Festival
8. 用	yòng	(v.)	use
9. 东西	dōngxi	(n.)	thing; stuff
10. 礼物	lǐwù	(n.)	present; gift
11. 去年	qùnián	(n.)	last year
12. 收到	shōu dào		receive; get
13. 多	duō	(adj.)	many; much
14. 压岁钱	yāsuìqián	(n.)	money given to children as a lunar New Year gift

Wang Jiaming is talking about the Spring Festival with Jack.

杰克：今天这里很热闹，为什么？
jié kè jīn tiān zhè lǐ hěn rè nao wèi shén me

家明：因为后天是春节，大家都买年货。
jiā míng yīn wèi hòu tiān shì chūn jié dà jiā dōu mǎi nián huò

杰克：什么是年货？
jié kè shén me shì nián huò

家明：年货是过年的时候吃的和用的东西。
jiā míng nián huò shì guò nián de shí hou chī de hé yòng de dōng xi

杰克：过年的时候有没有礼物？
jié kè guò nián de shí hou yǒu méi yǒu lǐ wù

家明：有啊。去年我收到很多礼物，还收到很多压岁钱。
jiā míng yǒu a qù nián wǒ shōu dào hěn duō lǐ wù hái shōu dào hěn duō yā suì qián

Read aloud

很 多 礼 物 hěn duō lǐ wù	春 节 的 时 候 chūn jié de shí hou
很 多 东 西 hěn duō dōng xi	过 年 的 时 候 guò nián de shí hou
很 多 压 岁 钱 hěn duō yā suì qián	吃 饭 的 时 候 chī fàn de shí hou

On your own: Make conversations according to the given words.

A：这 里 很 热 闹，为 什 么？
zhè lǐ hěn rè nao wèishén me

B：因 为 后 天 是 春 节。
yīn wèi hòu tiān shì chūn jié

1. 他 们 家 很 热 闹 今 天 是 春 节
tā men jiā hěn rè nao jīn tiān shì chūn jié

2. 他 很 高 兴 他 收 到 很 多 礼 物
tā hěn gāoxìng tā shōudào hěn duō lǐ wù

3. 她 很 高 兴 她 收 到 很 多 压 岁 钱
tā hěn gāoxìng tā shōudào hěn duō yā suì qián

Interview your partners

1. 过 年 的 时 候，你 们 家 买 年 货 吗？
guò nián de shí hou nǐ men jiā mǎi nián huò ma

2. 爸 爸 妈 妈 给 你 压 岁 钱 吗？
bà ba mā ma gěi nǐ yā suì qián ma

3. 你 喜 欢 过 年 吗？为 什 么？
nǐ xǐ huan guò nián ma wèi shén me

Class activity

1. What are the similarities and differences in how people celebrate Spring Festival and Christmas?

春 节
families get together
give children money as a gift
...

圣诞节
families get together
give children gifts
...

2. Chinese families usually decorate the windows with paper-cuts during Spring Festival. These paper-cuts are all made by hand. Why don't you try to make some of your own paper-cuts?

Phonetics

1. Listen to the tape, and then answer the following questions.

(1) Why does the boy buy a cake?

(2) Does he buy any gifts for his mother?

(3) What gift does he buy?

2. Read aloud the following children's song.

新年到，新年到，
xīn nián dào xīn nián dào

穿新衣，戴新帽，
chuān xīn yī dài xīn mào

吃饺子，放花炮，
chī jiǎo zi fàng huā pào

新年、新年真热闹！
xīn nián xīn nián zhēn rè nao

New Year is here. New Year is here.

We have new clothes and hats to wear.

A time to make dumplings and set off firecrackers.

What a lively and crazy New Year!

Learn to write

1. Structure of Chinese characters

为	用	东	西
礼	物	收	买
后	过	闹	因

2. Examples of components

部件 bù jiàn	甲骨文 jiǎ gǔ wén	金文 jīn wén	小篆 xiǎo zhuàn	楷书 kǎi shū	组字 zǔ zì
牜				牛	物
口				口	因
攵				攵	收

27 一共多少钱

yí gòng duō shao qián

Look and Say

果 酱
guǒ jiàng

黄 油
huáng yóu

口 香 糖
kǒu xiāngtáng

面 包
miàn bāo

New words

1. 盒	hé	(m.)	box
2. 牛奶	niúnǎi	(n.)	milk
3. 瓶	píng	(m.)	bottle
4. 果酱	guǒjiàng	(n.)	jam
5. 块	kuài	(m.)	lump; piece ①
6. 黄油	huángyóu	(n.)	butter
7. 面包	miànbāo	(n.)	bread
8. 别的	biéde	(pron.)	else; other; another
9. 包	bāo	(m.)	measure word ②
10. 口香糖	kǒuxiāngtáng	(n.)	chewing gum
11. 一共	yígòng	(adv.)	altogether
12. 找	zhǎo	(v.)	give change

① Used of sth. cubical or flat in shape.

② Used of bunddled or packaged things.

Wang Jiaming is shopping.

店员：您好，您买什么？
diàn yuán nín hǎo nín mǎi shén me

家明：我买一盒牛奶、一瓶果酱、三块黄油和两个面包。
jiā míng wǒ mǎi yì hé niú nǎi yì píng guǒ jiàng sān kuài huáng yóu hé liǎng ge miàn bāo

店员：还要别的东西吗？
diàn yuán hái yào bié de dōng xi ma

家明：还要一包口香糖。一共多少钱？
jiā míng hái yào yì bāo kǒu xiāng táng yí gòng duō shao qián

店员：一共十二元。
diàn yuán yí gòng shí èr yuán

店员：这是一百元，找您八十八元。
diàn yuán zhè shì yì bǎi yuán zhǎo nín bā shí bā yuán

Read and match

两 碗 汤
liǎng wǎn tāng

一 块 黄 油
yí kuài huáng yóu

两 瓶 果 酱
liǎng píng guǒ jiàng

一 盒 牛 奶
yì hé niú nǎi

两 个 面 包
liǎng ge miàn bāo

一 百 元 钱
yì bǎi yuán qián

四 个 饺 子
sì ge jiǎo zi

两 包 口 香 糖
liǎng bāo kǒu xiāng táng

Conversation practice: Substitute the alternate words to make a new dialogue.

A：一 共 多 少 钱？
yí gòng duō shao qián

B：一 共 48元，这 是 50元，找 您 2元。
yí gòng yuán zhè shì yuán zhǎo nín yuán

1. 55元 100元 45元
2. 69元 70元 1元
3. 88元 100元 12元

Calculations: Read the result out loud in Chinese.

20 − 11 =　　　50 − 13 =　　　100 − 78 =　　　80 − 59 =

Class activity: Going shopping.

Come to think of it, what do you need since your refrigerator is almost empty? Make a shopping list.

Phonetics

1. Listen to the tape, and then answer the following questions.

(1) What does the boy buy?

(2) How much does he spend on these things?

2. Read aloud the following riddle and make a guess.

双	手	抓	不	起，
shuāng	shǒu	zhuā	bù	qǐ
大	刀	劈	不	开。
dà	dāo	pī	bù	kāi
做	饭	和	洗	衣，
zuò	fàn	hé	xǐ	yī
都	要	请	它	来。
dōu	yào	qǐng	tā	lái

You can neither hold it in your hand nor cut it in half with a knife, but you cannot do without it when cooking and washing.

Learn to write

1. Structure of Chinese characters

牛	果	共	块
油	别	糖	瓶
盒	香	酱	

2. Examples of components

部件 bù jiàn	甲骨文 jiǎ gǔ wén	金文 jīn wén	小篆 xiǎo zhuàn	楷书 kǎi shū	组字 zǔ zì
土				土	块
由				由	油
另				另	别
唐				唐	糖
酉				酉	酱
瓦				瓦	瓶

你喜欢什么颜色

nǐ xǐ huan shén me yán sè

Look and Say

New words

1. 颜色	yánsè	(n.)	color
2. 蓝色	lánsè	(n.)	blue
3. 大海	dàhǎi	(n.)	sea; ocean
4. 绿色	lǜsè	(n.)	green
5. 树木	shùmù	(n.)	tree
6. 草地	cǎodì	(n.)	grassland
7. 红色	hóngsè	(n.)	red
8. 橙色	chéngsè	(n.)	orange
9. 种	zhǒng	(m.)	kind; sort; type
10. 明亮	míngliàng	(adj.)	bright

David, Mary and Wang Jiaming are watching a fashion show.

大卫：你喜欢什么颜色？
dà wèi nǐ xǐ huan shén me yán sè

玛丽：我喜欢蓝色，蓝色是大海的颜色。你呢？
mǎ lì wǒ xǐ huan lán sè lán sè shì dà hǎi de yán sè nǐ ne

大卫：我喜欢绿色。
dà wèi wǒ xǐ huan lǜ sè

玛丽：为什么？
mǎ lì wèi shén me

大卫：因为树木、草地都是绿色的。家明呢，你喜欢什么颜色？
dà wèi yīn wèi shù mù cǎo dì dōu shì lǜ sè de jiā míng ne nǐ xǐ huan shén me yán sè

家明：我喜欢红色和橙色，这两种颜色很明亮。
jiā míng wǒ xǐ huan hóng sè hé chéng sè zhè liǎng zhǒng yán sè hěn míng liàng

On your own: Ask and answer questions based on the following pictures.

Example

A：树木是什么颜色的？
shù mù shì shén me yán sè de

B：树木是绿色的。
shù mù shì lǜ sè de

大海
dà hǎi

草地
cǎo dì

钱包
qián bāo

文具盒
wén jù hé

雨伞
yǔ sǎn

Conversation practice: Substitute the alternate words to make a new dialogue.

A：你喜欢什么颜色？
nǐ xǐ huan shén me yán sè

B：我喜欢绿色。
wǒ xǐ huan lǜ sè

A：为什么？
wèi shén me

B：因为绿色是草地的颜色。
yīn wèi lǜ sè shì cǎo dì de yán sè

1. 红色 hóng sè — 红色很明亮 hóng sè hěn míng liàng
2. 橙色 chéng sè — 橙色很漂亮 chéng sè hěn piào liang
3. 蓝色 lán sè — 蓝色是天空的颜色 lán sè shì tiān kōng de yán sè

Interview your friends

1. 你喜欢什么颜色？为什么？
nǐ xǐ huan shén me yán sè wèi shén me
2. 你爸爸妈妈喜欢什么颜色？
nǐ bà ba mā ma xǐ huan shén me yán sè
3. 你的汉语老师喜欢什么颜色？
nǐ de hàn yǔ lǎo shī xǐ huan shén me yán sè
4. 你的朋友们喜欢什么颜色？
nǐ de péng you men xǐ huan shén me yán sè

Class activity

A maze of color (see the appendix).

Phonetics

1. Listen to the tape, and then answer the following questions.

(1) What color does the girl like? Why?

(2) What color does the boy like ?Why?

2. Read aloud the following Chinese ancient poem.

鹅，鹅，鹅，
é é é

曲 项 向 天 歌。
qū xiàng xiàng tiān gē

白 毛 浮 绿 水，
bái máo fú lǜ shuǐ

红 掌 拨 清 波。
hóng zhǎng bō qīng bō

Geese, geese, geese,

singing into the sky with curving necks.

White feather floating on the turquoise water,

red pads playing with crystal ripples.

Learn to write

1. Structure of Chinese characters

木	颜	海	绿
地	红	橙	色
草	蓝	树	

2. Examples of components

部件 bù jiàn	甲骨文 jiǎ gǔ wén	金文 jīn wén	小篆 xiǎo zhuàn	楷书 kǎi shū	组字 zǔ zì
页				页(頁)	颜
录				录	绿
工				工	红
纟				糸	绿

29 穿这件还是穿那件

chuān zhè jiàn hái shi chuān nà jiàn

Look and Say

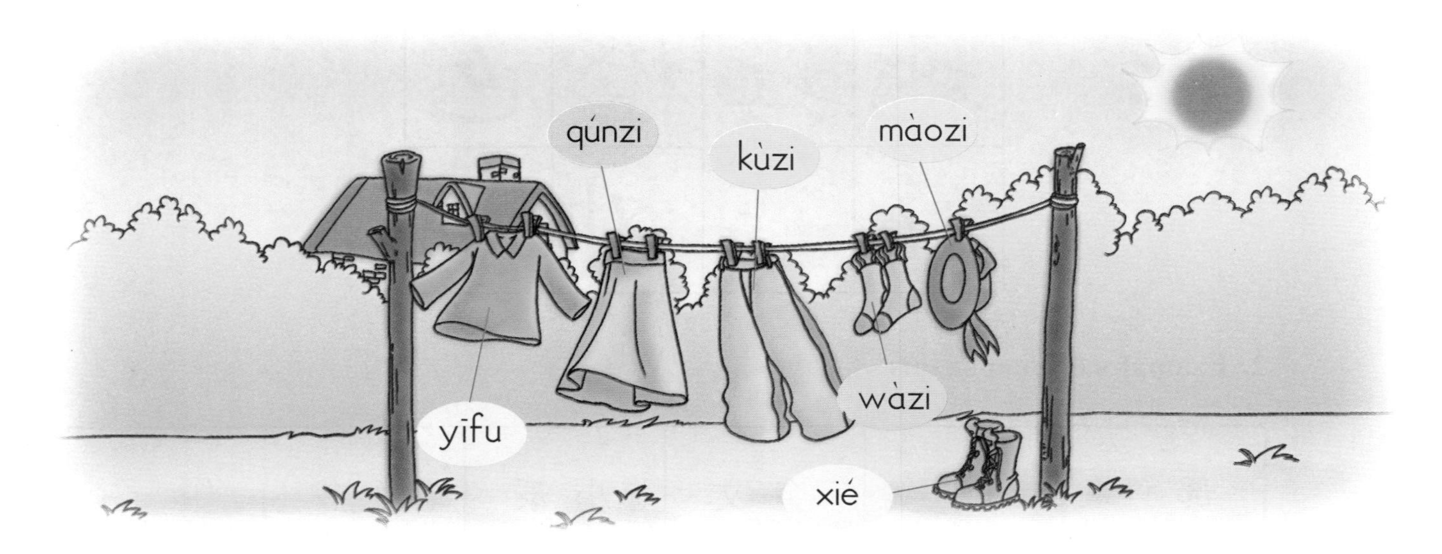

New words

1. 件	jiàn	(m.)	piece ①
2. 衣服	yīfu	(n.)	clothes
3. 不错	búcuò	(adj.)	not bad
4. 穿	chuān	(v.)	wear
5. 还是	háishi	(conj.)	or
6. 如果	rúguǒ	(conj.)	if
7. 配	pèi	(v.)	match; go well with
8. 黑色	hēisè	(n.)	black
9. 裙子	qúnzi	(n.)	dress

① Mainly used of clothes or matters.

Mary is going to a party and she is asking her mother which dress she should wear.

玛 丽：妈 妈，这 件 衣 服 怎 么 样？
mǎ lì mā ma zhè jiàn yī fu zěn me yàng

妈 妈：这 件 衣 服 很 漂 亮。
mā ma zhè jiàn yī fu hěn piào liang

玛 丽：那 件 呢？
mǎ lì nà jiàn ne

妈 妈：那 件 也 不 错。
mā ma nà jiàn yě bú cuò

玛 丽：今 天 我 穿 哪 件？穿 这 件 还 是 穿 那 件？
mǎ lì jīn tiān wǒ chuān nǎ jiàn chuān zhè jiàn hái shi chuān nà jiàn

妈 妈：如 果 配 黑 色 的 裙 子，这 件 不 好，那 件 好。
mā ma rú guǒ pèi hēi sè de qún zi zhè jiàn bù hǎo nà jiàn hǎo

On your own: Ask and answer questions based on the following pictures.

1. A：这 件 衣 服 怎 么 样？
zhè jiàn yī fu zěn me yàng

B：这 件 衣 服 很 漂 亮。
zhè jiàn yī fu hěn piào liang

1. 条 tiáo	红 裙 子 hóng qún zi	很 不 错 hěn bú cuò
2. 条 tiáo	黑 裙 子 hēi qún zi	也 很 漂 亮 yě hěn piào liang

2. A：你 喜 欢 红 色 还 是 蓝 色？
nǐ xǐ huan hóng sè hái shi lán sè

B：我 喜 欢 红 色。
wǒ xǐ huan hóng sè

1. 绿 色 lǜ sè	黑 色 hēi sè
2. 红 色 hóng sè	橙 色 chéng sè

Class activity

1. Fashion designer

Have you ever tried to design any clothes? Design an outlit, complete with colors, then use Chinese to describe it to your classmates.

裤子	kùzi	pants
鞋子	xiézi	shoes
帽子	màozi	hat
袜子	wàzi	socks

2. Partiality for colors

Check your wardrobe and write down the colors of all your clothes. What color predominates your wardrobe? Is it your favorite color? Exchange what you have written down with your friends and ask for their suggestions on the colors of your clothing.

Phonetics

1. Listen to the tape, and then answer the following questions.

(1) Which clothes does the boy think looks good? Why?

(2) What color does the boy think matches the red dress?

2. Read aloud the following tongue twister.

小 方 和 小 黄，
xiǎo fāng hé xiǎo huáng

一 起 画 凤 凰。
yì qǐ huà fèng huáng

小 方 画 黄 凤 凰，
xiǎo fāng huà huáng fèng huáng

小 黄 画 红 凤 凰。
xiǎo huáng huà hóng fèng huáng

红 凤 凰 和 黄 凤 凰，
hóng fèng huáng hé huáng fèng huáng

样 子 都 像 活 凤 凰。
yàng zi dōu xiàng huó fèng huáng

Xiao Fang and Xiao Huang are competing in drawing a phoenix.

Xiao Fang is drawing a yellow phoenix.

Xiao Huang is drawing a red phoenix.

Red phoenix and yellow phoenix are both like real phoenixes.

Learn to write

1. Structure of Chinese characters

衣	件	服	错	如
配	裙	穿	黑	

2. Examples of components

部件 bù jiàn	甲骨文 jiǎ gǔ wén	金文 jīn wén	小篆 xiǎo zhuàn	楷书 kǎi shū	组字 zǔ zì
衤				衣	裙
穴				穴	穿
己				己	配
昔				昔	错

他什么样子

tā shén me yàng zi

Look and Say

CAN YOU DESCRIBE THESE PEOPLE?

New words

1. 样子	yàngzi	(n.)	appearance; look
2. 辆	liàng	(m.)	measure word ①
3. 白色	báisè	(n.)	white
4. 男	nán	(adj.)	man
5. 头发	tóufa	(n.)	hair
6. 长	cháng	(adj.)	long
7. 戴	dài	(v.)	(of glasses, hats) wear
8. 副	fù	(m.)	pair; set
9. 墨镜	mòjìng	(n.)	dark glasses; sunglasses
10. 黄色	huángsè	(n.)	yellow
11. 紫色	zǐsè	(n.)	purple
12. 车牌	chēpái	(n.)	licence plate
13. 号码	hàomǎ	(n.)	number

Wang Jiaming was the victim of a hit-and-run accident. The policeman asked him to describe the car and the driver, so Wang Jiaming gave the following description.

那辆车是白色的。开车的人是男的，头发很长，戴一副墨镜，穿黄色的衣服，紫色的裤子。车牌号码是 FC59633。

Nà liàng chē shì báisè de. Kāichē de rén shì nán de, tóufa hěn cháng, dài yí fù mòjìng, chuān huángsè de yīfu, zǐsè de kùzi. Chēpái hàomǎ shì FC59633.

① Used with vehicles.

Read aloud

男的
nán de

女的
nǚ de

长头发
cháng tóu fa

短头发
duǎn tóu fa

一辆黑色的汽车
yí liàng hēi sè de qì chē

一副墨镜
yí fù mò jìng

一条紫色的裤子
yì tiáo zǐ sè de kù zi

一件红色的衣服
yí jiàn hóng sè de yī fu

On your own: Ask and answer questions based on the following pictures.

1. A：那辆车是白色的吗？
nà liàng chē shì bái sè de ma

B：对，是白色的。
duì shì bái sè de

1. 车牌号码　FC59633
chē pái hào mǎ

2. 开车的人　男的
kāi chē de rén　nán de

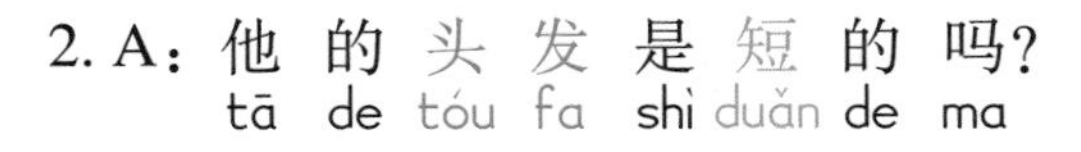

2. A：他的头发是短的吗？
tā de tóu fa shì duǎn de ma

B：不，他的头发是长的。
bù tā de tóu fa shì cháng de

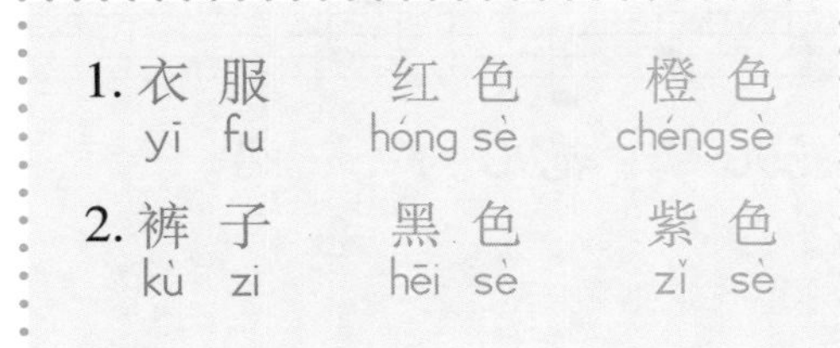

1. 衣服　红色　橙色
yī fu　hóng sè　chéng sè

2. 裤子　黑色　紫色
kù zi　hēi sè　zǐ sè

Phonetics

1. Listen to the tape, and then answer the following questions.

(1) What does the man the girl asks about buy?

(2) What color are the jacket and pants the man wears?

(3) What color is the man's hair?

2. Read aloud the following children's song.

小 小 姑 娘 清 早 起 床，
xiǎo xiǎo gū niang qīng zǎo qǐ chuáng

提 着 花 篮 上 市 场，
tí zhe huā lán shàng shì chǎng

穿 过 大 街，走 过 小 巷，
chuān guò dà jiē zǒu guò xiǎo xiàng

卖 花 儿 卖 花 儿 声 声 唱。
mài huār mài huār shēng shēng chàng

A little girl got up early in the morning. She went to the market with a basket of flowers for selling. Going through streets and lanes so zigzagging, "flowers for selling" was what she was singing.

Can you sing it?

Learn to write

1. Structure of Chinese characters

白	头	长	发	开
辆	副	镜	牌	码
男	紫	墨	戴	

2. Examples of components

部件 bù jiàn	甲骨文 jiǎ gǔ wén	金文 jīn wén	小篆 xiǎo zhuàn	楷书 kǎi shū	组字 zǔ zì
车			車	车(車)	辆
片				片	牌
田				田	男
力				力	男
糸				糸	紫

UNIT SUMMARY

FUNCTIONAL USAGE

1. Ordering food in a restaurant

我 要 二 十 个 饺 子。
wǒ yào èr shí ge jiǎo zi

我 要 一 碗 鸡 蛋 汤。
wǒ yào yì wǎn jī dàn tāng

2. Inquiring about and giving reasons

今 天 这 里 很 热 闹，
jīn tiān zhè lǐ hěn rè nao

为 什 么？
wèi shén me

因 为 后 天 是 春 节，
yīn wèi hòu tiān shì chūn jié

大 家 都 买 年 货。
dà jiā dōu mǎi nián huò

3. Inquiring about and telling about the sum of money

一 共 多 少 钱？
yí gòng duō shao qián

一 共 十 二 元。
yí gòng shí èr yuán

4. Inquiring about and telling about one's favorite color

你 喜 欢 什 么 颜 色？
nǐ xǐ huan shén me yán sè

我 喜 欢 蓝 色。
wǒ xǐ huan lán sè

5. Asking for others' opinion on something

我 穿 这 件 还 是
wǒ chuān zhè jiàn hái shi

穿 那 件？
chuān nà jiàn

6. Describing the features of someone

开 车 的 人 是 男 的，
kāi chē de rén shì nán de

头 发 很 长，戴 一 副
tóu fa hěn cháng, dài yí fù

墨 镜。
mò jìng

GRAMMAR FOCUS

Sentence pattern	*Example*
1. (一) 点 儿 yì diǎnr	您 吃 点 儿 什 么? nín chī diǎnr shén me
2. 因 为…… yīn wèi	因 为 后 天 是 春 节, yīn wèi hòu tiān shì chūn jié 大 家 都 买 年 货。 dà jiā dōu mǎi nián huò
3. V. + 什 么 shén me	您 买 什 么? nín mǎi shén me
4. ……还 是…… hái shi	今 天 我 穿 这 件 还 是 穿 那 jīn tiān wǒ chuān zhè jiàn hái shi chuān nà 件? jiàn
5. 如 果…… rú guǒ	如 果 配 黑 色 的 裙 子, rú guǒ pèi hēi sè de qún zi 这 件 不 好, 那 件 好。 zhè jiàn bù hǎo nà jiàn hǎo
6. 是……的 shì de	那 辆 车 是 白 色 的。 nà liàng chē shì bái sè de

Unit Six

Sports and Health

Look and Say

31 你哪儿不舒服

nǐ nǎr bù shū fu

Look and Say

New words

1. 疼	téng	(v.)	ache; hurt
2. 左	zuǒ	(n.)	left
3. 腿	tuǐ	(n.)	leg
4. 舒服	shūfu	(adj.)	be well; comfortable
5. 头	tóu	(n.)	head
6. 有点儿	yǒudiǎnr	(adv.)	a bit; rather ①
7. 检查	jiǎnchá	(v.)	examine; check
8. 一下儿	yíxiàr		once ②
9. 身体	shēntǐ	(n.)	health; body
10. 问题	wèntí	(n.)	problem
11. 药	yào	(n.)	medicine
12. 休息	xiūxi	(v.)	rest

① Usu. used of sth. unfavorable.

② Used after a verb, indicating an act or an attempt.

Wang Jiaming gets examined at the emergency room.

医生：你哪儿疼？
yī shēng nǐ nǎr téng

家明：我左腿疼。
jiā míng wǒ zuǒ tuǐ téng

医生：还有哪儿不舒服？
yī shēng hái yǒu nǎr bù shū fu

家明：我的头有点儿疼。
jiā míng wǒ de tóu yǒu diǎnr téng

医生：好，我检查一下儿。你的身体没有大问题，吃点儿药，休息一天吧。
yī shēng hǎo wǒ jiǎn chá yí xiàr nǐ de shēn tǐ méi yǒu dà wèn tí chī diǎnr yào xiū xi yì tiān ba

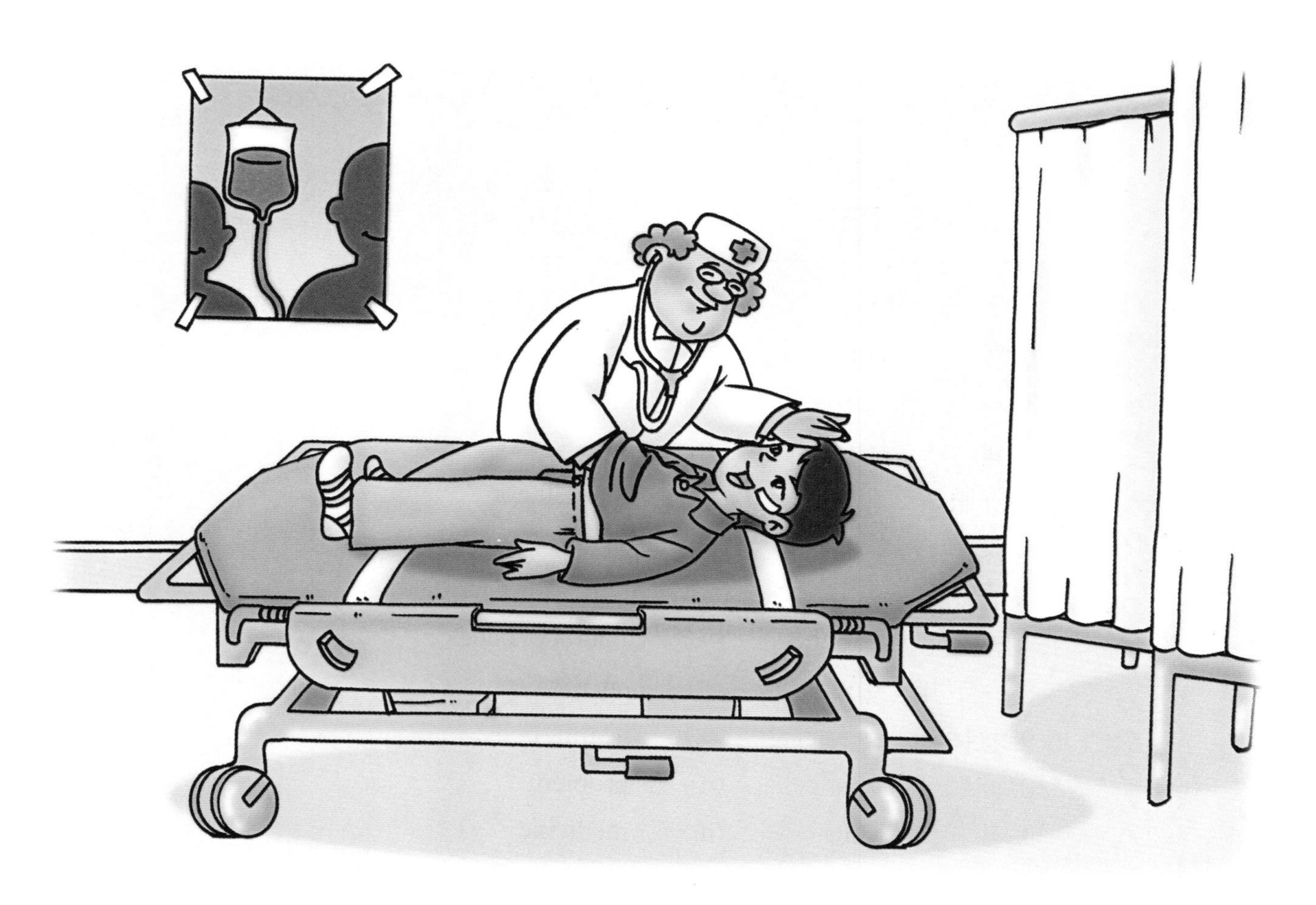

Answer the following questions.

1. 王家明的身体怎么样？
   wáng jiā míng de shēn tǐ zěn me yàng
2. 他哪儿疼？
   tā nǎr téng
3. 他哪儿不舒服？
   tā nǎr bù shū fu

Where does he hurt?

Tā nǎr téng?

他头疼、眼睛疼、耳朵疼、肚子疼，他的腿也疼。他很不舒服。
tā tóuténg yǎn jingténg ěr duoténg dù zi téng tā de tuǐ yě téng tā hěn bù shū fu

On your own: Ask and answer questions based on the following pictures.

A: 你哪儿不舒服？
nǐ nǎr bù shū fu

B: 我的头有点儿疼。
wǒ de tóu yǒu diǎnr téng

头
tóu

腿
tuǐ

Class activity: Doctor, doctor, I need help...

Students get in groups of 5-6. One acts as the doctor and others as patients.

Phonetics

1. Listen to the tape, and then answer the following questions.

(1) What does the woman do?

(2) What is wrong with the man?

(3) What does the woman suggest the man do?

2. Read aloud the following tongue twister.

吃	葡	萄	不	吐	葡	萄	皮	儿，	
chī	pú	tao	bù	tǔ	pú	tao	pír		
不	吃	葡	萄	倒	吐	葡	萄	皮	儿。
bù	chī	pú	tao	dào	tǔ	pú	tao	pír	

Eating grapes without spitting out their skin,
yet without eating grapes spitting out the skin.

Learn to write

1. Structure of Chinese characters

身	舒	检	体	休
腿	查	息	药	疼
题				

2. Examples of components

部件 bù jiàn	甲骨文 jiǎ gǔ wén	金文 jīn wén	小篆 xiǎo zhuàn	楷书 kǎi shū	组字 zǔ zì
疒				疒	疼
佥				佥(僉)	检
本				本	体
是				是	题

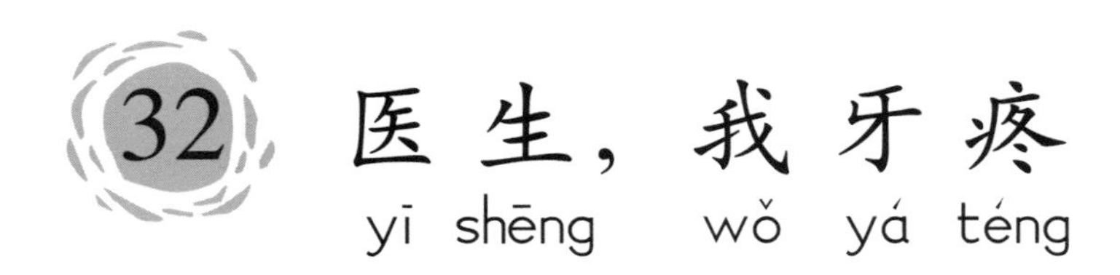

32 医生，我牙疼
yī shēng wǒ yá téng

Look and Say

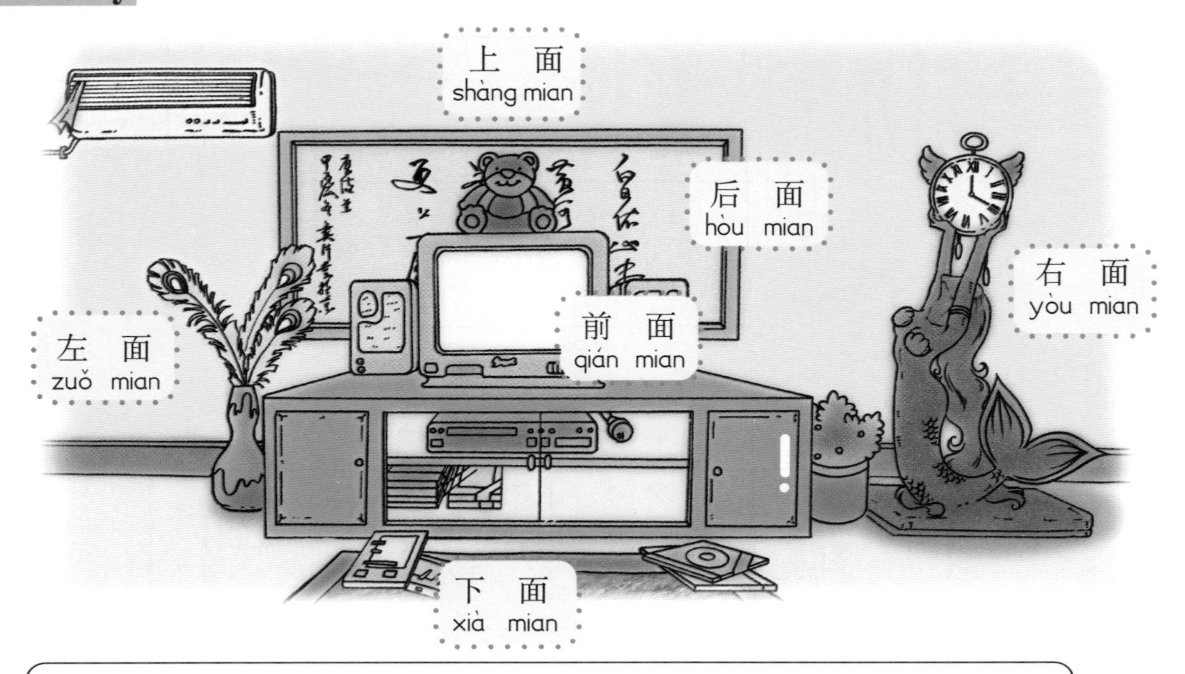

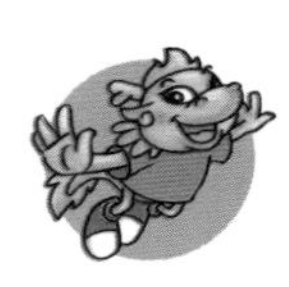

New words

1. 牙	yá	(n.)	tooth
2. 颗	kē	(m.)	measure word ①
3. 上面	shàngmian	(n.)	upper part
4. 下面	xiàmian	(n.)	lower part
5. 右边	yòubian	(n.)	right
6. 第	dì	(af.)	prefix ②
7. 糟糕	zāogāo	(adj.)	terrible; too bad
8. 糖	táng	(n.)	candy
9. 特别	tèbié	(adv.)	specially
10. 巧克力	qiǎokèlì	(n.)	chocolate
11. 以后	yǐhòu	(n.)	afterwards; after; later
12. 应该	yīnggāi	(v.; aux.)	should
13. 少	shǎo	(adj.)	few; little

① Used of grains and grain-like things.

② Indicating ordinal numbers.

Jack is talking with his dentist.

杰 克：医 生，我 牙 疼！
jié kè yī shēng wǒ yá téng

医 生：哪 一 颗 牙，上 面 的 还 是 下 面 的？
yī shēng nǎ yì kē yá shàng mian de hái shi xià mian de

杰 克：下 面 的。
jié kè xià mian de

医 生：左 边 还 是 右 边？
yī shēng zuǒ bian hái shi yòu bian

杰 克：右 边 第 三 颗。
jié kè yòu bian dì sān kē

医 生：你 的 牙 很 糟 糕。你 是 不 是 喜 欢 吃 糖？
yī shēng nǐ de yá hěn zāo gāo nǐ shì bu shì xǐ huan chī táng

杰 克：对，我 特 别 喜 欢 吃 巧 克 力。
jié kè duì wǒ tè bié xǐ huan chī qiǎo kè lì

医 生：以 后 应 该 少 吃。
yī shēng yǐ hòu yīng gāi shǎo chī

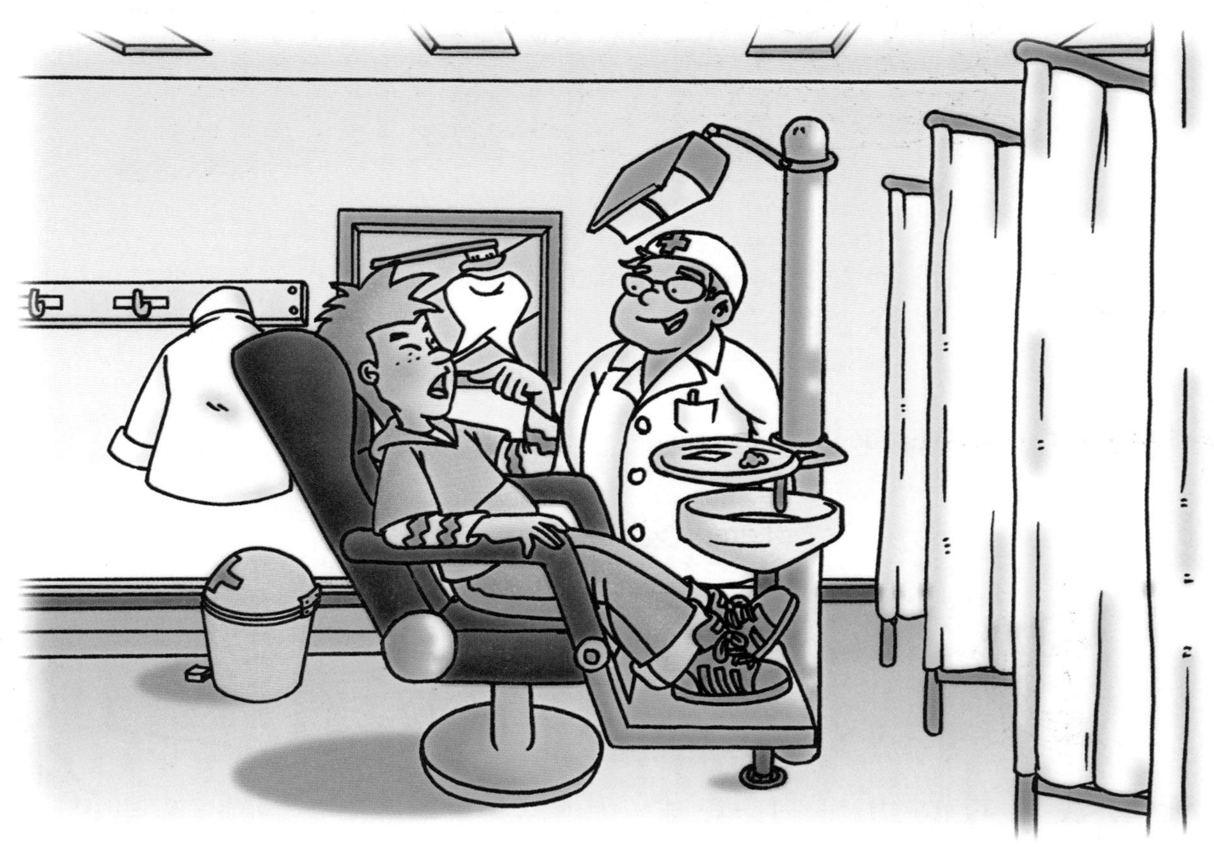

Act it out

上——上，下——下，
shàng shàng xià xià

左——左，右——右，
zuǒ zuǒ yòu yòu

前——前，后——后，
qián qián hòu hòu

我 们 都 是 好 朋 友。
wǒ men dōu shì hǎo péng you

Read and match

第二个 dì èr ge	第五个 dì wǔ ge	第一个 dì yī ge	第四个 dì sì ge	第七个 dì qī ge	第三个 dì sān ge	第六个 dì liù ge

On your own: What do they like to do?

Tāmen xǐhuan gàn shénme?

他 喜 欢 吃 巧 克 力。
tā xǐ huan chī qiǎo kè lì

打 篮 球
dǎ lán qiú

开 车
kāi chē

看 电 影
kàn diànyǐng

Interview your partners

1. 你 喜 欢 干 什 么?
   nǐ xǐ huan gàn shén me

2. 你 的 朋 友 们 喜 欢 干 什 么?
   nǐ de péng you men xǐ huan gàn shén me

Class activity

Find out how many of your classmates have had a toothache. Discuss why they might have gotten a toothache and come up with suggestions on how they might avoid them in the future.

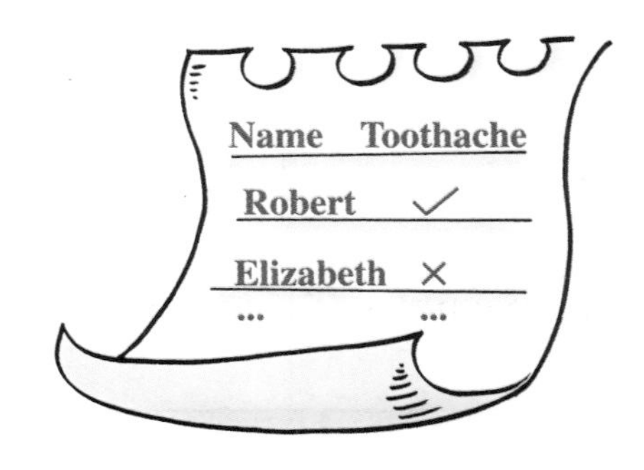

Phonetics

1. Listen to the tape, and then answer the following questions.

(1) What's wrong with the girl?

(2) Which of her teeth is aching?

(3) Does she have any other problems?

2. Read aloud the following riddle and make a guess.

远 看 山 有 色，
yuǎn kàn shān yǒu sè

近 听 水 无 声。
jìn tīng shuǐ wú shēng

春 去 花 还 在，
chūn qù huā hái zài

人 来 鸟 不 惊。
rén lái niǎo bù jīng

Being looked at from the distance the mountain is colored; the water runs in silence however close you're to it for a listening. The flowers are still in blossoms even when spring has gone; the birds won't flow away when you're coming.

Learn to write

1. Structure of Chinese characters

牙	力	颗	糟	特
巧	该	第	应	边

2. Examples of components

部件 bù jiàn	甲骨文 jiǎ gǔ wén	金文 jīn wén	小篆 xiǎo zhuàn	楷书 kǎi shū	组字 zǔ zì
果				果	颗
寺				寺	特
弗				弗	第
曹				曹	糟

33 你会游泳吗

nǐ huì yóu yǒng ma

Look and Say

New words

1. 经常 jīngcháng (adv.) often
2. 锻炼 duànliàn (v.) do exercises
3. 运动 yùndòng (n.) sports
4. 跑步 pǎobù (v.) jogging
5. 游泳 yóuyǒng (v.) swim
6. 会 huì (v.; aux.) can
7. 要是 yàoshi (conj.) if
8. 时间 shíjiān (n.) time
9. 教 jiāo (v.) teach

Mary and Wang Jiaming are talking about exercising.

玛　丽：家　明，你　经　常　锻　炼　身　体　吗？
mǎ　lì　jiā　míng　nǐ　jīng cháng duàn liàn shēn　tǐ　ma

家　明：不　经　常　锻　炼。
jiā　míng　bù　jīng cháng duàn liàn

玛　丽：你　喜　欢　什　么　运　动？
mǎ　lì　nǐ　xǐ　huan shén　me　yùn dòng

家　明：我　喜　欢　跑　步。你　呢？
jiā　míng　wǒ　xǐ　huan pǎo　bù　nǐ　ne

玛　丽：我　喜　欢　游　泳。你　会　游　泳　吗？
mǎ　lì　wǒ　xǐ　huan yóu yǒng　nǐ　huì　yóu yǒng　ma

家　明：我　不　会。要　是　有　时　间，你　教　我　吧！
jiā　míng　wǒ　bú　huì　yào　shi　yǒu　shí　jiān　nǐ　jiāo　wǒ　ba

Answer the following questions according to the text.

1. 王 家 明 经 常 锻 炼 身 体 吗?
   wáng jiā míng jīngcháng duànliàn shēn tǐ ma
2. 玛 丽 喜 欢 什 么 运 动?
   mǎ lì xǐ huan shén me yùn dòng
3. 王 家 明 喜 欢 什 么 运 动?
   wáng jiā míng xǐ huan shén me yùn dòng
4. 谁 会 游 泳?
   shuí huì yóu yǒng

On your own: Make sentences according to the given words and pictures.

1. What do they usually do?

他 经 常 锻 炼 身 体。
tā jīngcháng duàn liàn shēn tǐ

看 电 影
kàn diànyǐng

买 东 西
mǎi dōng xi

吃 比 萨 饼
chī bǐ sà bǐng

2. What can they do?

他 会 打 乒 乓 球。
tā huì dǎ pīngpāng qiú

游 泳
yóu yǒng

打 网 球
dǎ wǎng qiú

开 车
kāi chē

Conversation practice: Substitute the alternate words to make a new dialogue.

A: 你 会 游 泳 吗?
nǐ huì yóuyǒngma

B: 会 啊, 我 很 喜 欢 游 泳。
huì a wǒ hěn xǐ huanyóuyǒng

A: 要 是 有 时 间, 你 教 我 游 泳 吧!
yào shi yǒu shí jiān nǐ jiāo wǒ yóuyǒngba

B: 好, 没 问 题!
hǎo méiwèn tí

1. 开 车 kāi chē
2. 打 网 球 dǎwǎng qiú
3. 滑 雪 huá xuě
4. 弹 吉 他 tán jí tā

Class activity

Interview your classmates and find out what their favorite sports are and how often they play them. Vote for the most popular sports and the sports star in your class.

Name	Favorite sports	Frequency
Diane	游泳	一周两次
Peter	滑板	一天一次
...	...	...

Phonetics

1. Listen to the tape, and then answer the following questions.

(1) Does the girl often do exercises?
(2) What is the girl's favorite sport?
(3) Can she play basketball?

2. Read aloud the following Chinese ancient poem.

清 明 时 节 雨 纷 纷,
qīng míng shí jié yǔ fēn fēn
路 上 行 人 欲 断 魂。
lù shang xíng rén yù duàn hún
借 问 酒 家 何 处 有,
jiè wèn jiǔ jiā hé chù yǒu
牧 童 遥 指 杏 花 村。
mù tóng yáo zhǐ xìng huā cūn

The day of mourning for the dead it's raining hard. My heart is broken on my way to the graveyard. Where can I find a wineshop to drown my sad hours? A herdboy points to a cot amid apricot flowers.

Learn to write

1. Structure of Chinese characters

经	炼	动	跑	教
泳	锻	游	步	会

2. Examples of components

部件 bù jiàn	甲骨文 jiǎ gǔ wén	金文 jīn wén	小篆 xiǎo zhuàn	楷书 kǎi shū	组字 zǔ zì
𢀖				𢀖(巠)	经
云				云	运 动
止				止	步
孝				孝	教

Look and Say

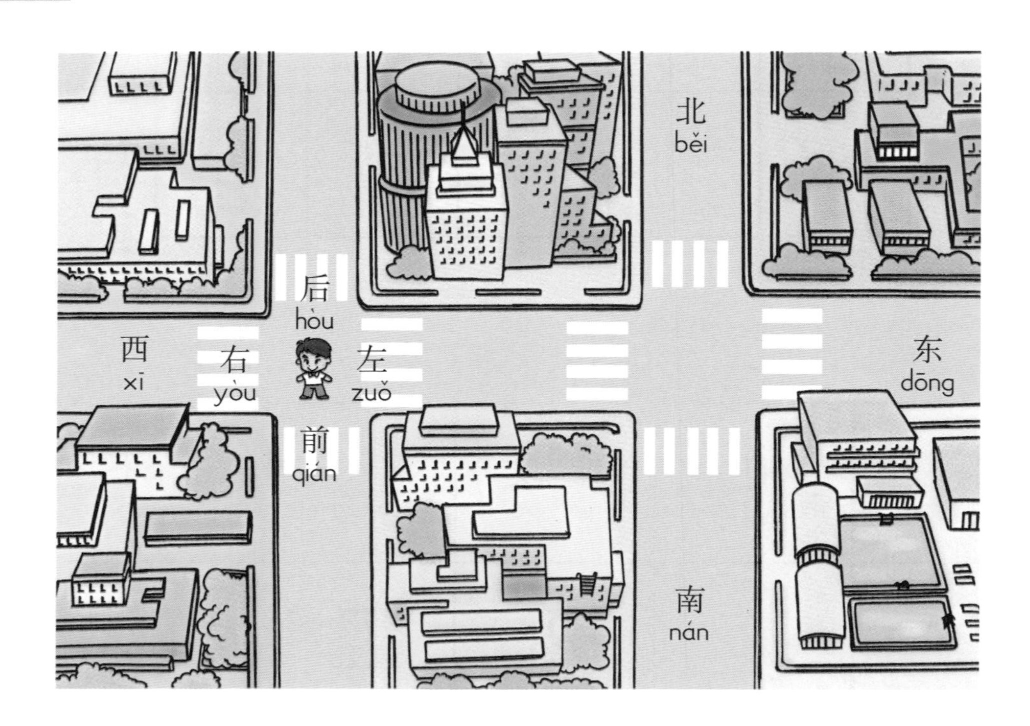

New words

1. 别	bié	(adv.)	don't
2. 担心	dānxīn	(v.)	worry
3. 游泳池	yóuyǒngchí	(n.)	swimming pool
4. 怎么	zěnme	(pron.)	how
5. 走	zǒu	(v.)	walk; get (to)
6. 向	xiàng	(prep.)	to; towards
7. 东	dōng	(n.)	east
8. 路口	lùkǒu	(n.)	crossing; junction; intersection
9. 右	yòu	(n.)	right
10. 拐	guǎi	(v.)	turn; change direction
11. 等	děng	(v.)	wait (for)

David is calling Wang Jiaming. They are going to swim.

大 卫：喂，我 是 大 卫。我 找 王 家 明。
dà wèi wèi wǒ shì dà wèi wǒ zhǎo wáng jiā míng

家 明：我 是 王 家 明。大 卫，你 好，什 么 事？
jiā míng wǒ shì wáng jiā míng dà wèi nǐ hǎo shén me shì

大 卫：你 去 不 去 游 泳？
dà wèi nǐ qù bu qù yóu yǒng

家 明：我 不 会 游 泳。
jiā míng wǒ bú huì yóu yǒng

大 卫：别 担 心，那 里 有 教 练。
dà wèi bié dān xīn nà li yǒu jiào liàn

家 明：好，我 去。去 游 泳 池 怎 么 走？
jiā míng hǎo wǒ qù qù yóu yǒng chí zěn me zǒu

大 卫：从 你 家 向 东 走，到 第 二 个 路 口 向 右 拐。
dà wèi cóng nǐ jiā xiàng dōng zǒu dào dì èr ge lù kǒu xiàng yòu guǎi

我 在 那 儿 等 你。
wǒ zài nàr děng nǐ

On your own

1. What are they doing?

他 们 在 干 什 么?
tā men zài gàn shén me

他 们 在 游 泳 池 游 泳。
tā men zài yóu yǒng chí yóu yǒng

她 们 饭 馆
tā men fàn guǎn

吃 比 萨 饼
chī bǐ sà bǐng

他 们 电 影 院
tā men diàn yǐng yuàn

看 电 影
kàn diàn yǐng

2. Make conversations according to the given words.

A: 今 天 有 雨。
jīn tiān yǒu yǔ

B: 别 担 心!
bié dān xīn

我 有 雨 伞。
wǒ yǒu yǔ sǎn

1. 不 会 游 泳
bú huì yóu yǒng

我 可 以 教 你
wǒ kě yǐ jiāo nǐ

2. 我 不 喜 欢 吃 比 萨 饼
wǒ bù xǐ huan chī bǐ sà bǐng

那 儿 还 有 饺 子
nàr hái yǒu jiǎo zi

Conversation practice

Now suppose you are on the eastside of Cypress Street and someone wants to go to the following places. Please tell him/her how to get there.

1. 比 萨 饼 店
bǐ sà bǐng diàn

2. 医 院
yī yuàn

3. 电 影 院
diàn yǐng yuàn

Example

A: 请 问，去 游 泳 池 怎 么 走?
qǐng wèn qù yóu yǒng chí zěn me zǒu

B: 向 东 走，到 第 二 个 路 口
xiàng dōng zǒu dào dì èr ge lù kǒu
向 右 拐。
xiàng yòu guǎi

A: 谢 谢 您!
xiè xie nín

B: 别 客 气!
bié kè qi

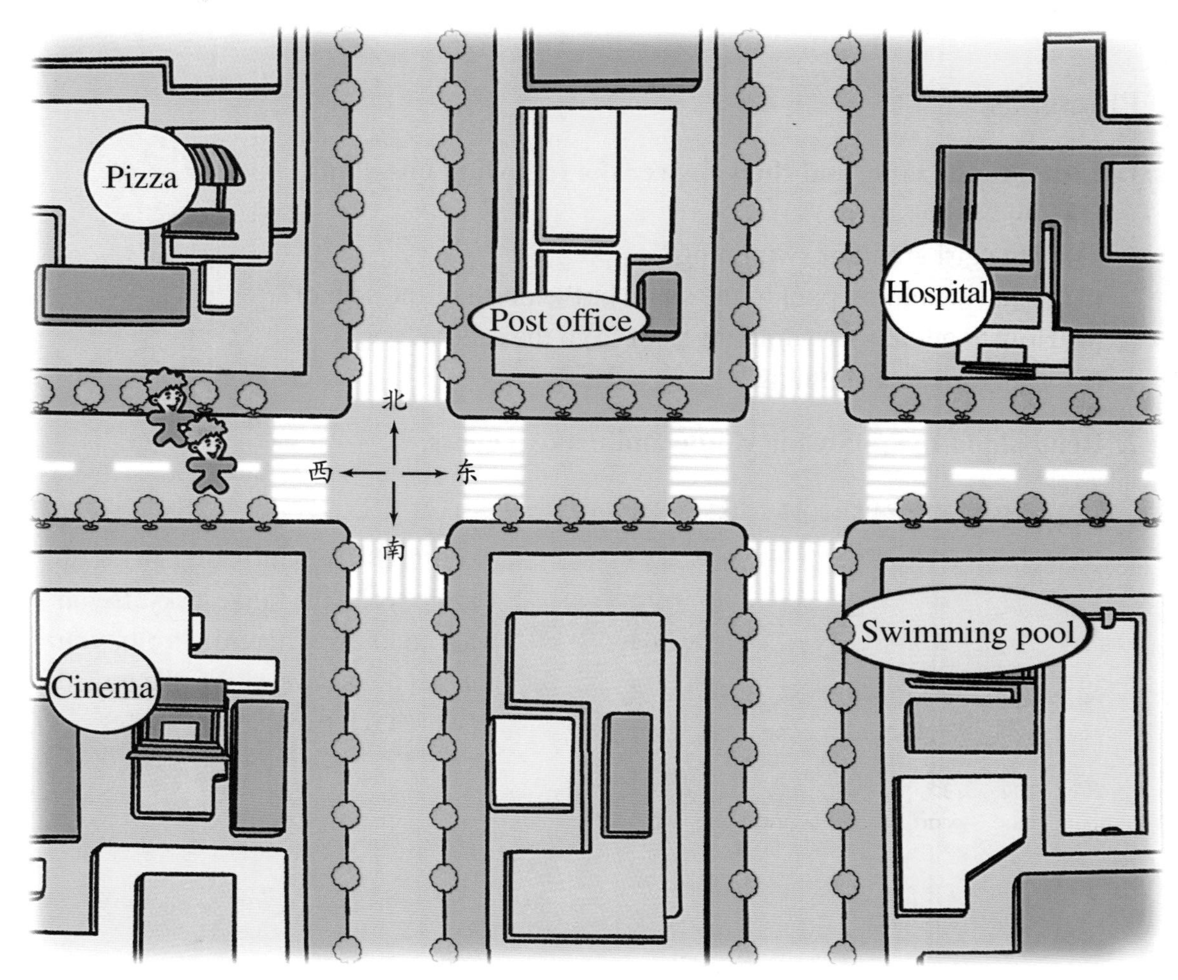

Class activity: Crazy sentences.

Every student makes up three different cards. The first will contain their names, the second will contain the name of a place and the third will contain the things they are going to do. The teacher will keep these cards in three separate piles and ask each student to come and randomly choose one card from each pile and make a sentence.

王家明

在游泳池里

吃比萨饼

Phonetics

1. Listen to the tape, and then answer the following questions.

(1) Can the girl swim?

(2) Is the girl afraid of swimming?

(3) Is the swimming pool to the south or the north of the school?

(4) How to get to the swimming pool from the school?

(5) Will Tom go swimming?

2. Read aloud the following riddle and make a guess.

一	只	蝴	蝶	轻	轻	飘，
yì	zhī	hú	dié	qīng	qīng	piāo
顺	风	直	上	九	重	霄。
shùn	fēng	zhí	shàng	jiǔ	chóng	xiāo
要	知	蝴	蝶	从	哪	来，
yào	zhī	hú	dié	cóng	nǎ	lái
顺	着	线	儿	往	下	找。
shùn	zhe	xiàn	er	wǎng	xià	zhǎo

A butterfly is fluttering briskly. High beyond the highest sky. If you want to know where it's from, you can get the answer along the thread to which it's tied.

Learn to write

1. Structure of Chinese characters

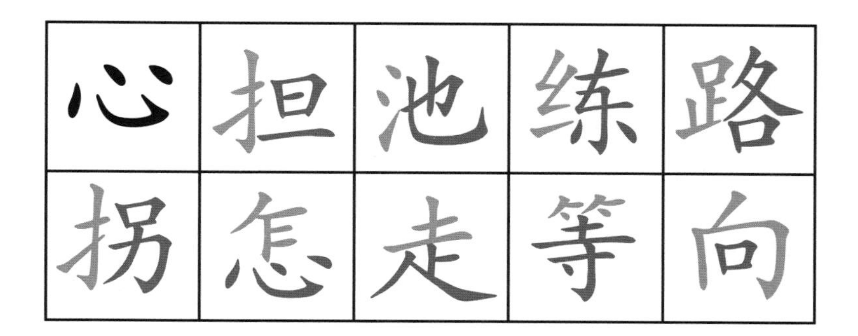

心	担	池	练	路
拐	怎	走	等	向

2. Examples of components

部件 bù jiàn	甲骨文 jiǎ gǔ wén	金文 jīn wén	小篆 xiǎo zhuàn	楷书 kǎi shū	组字 zǔ zì
旦				旦	担
各				各	路
东				东(東)	练

35 你去哪儿度暑假
nǐ qù nǎr dù shǔ jià

Look and Say

山区
shān qū

爬山
pá shān

海边
hǎi biān

游泳
yóu yǒng

New words

1. 度 dù (v.) spend (holidays)
2. 暑假 shǔjià (n.) summer vacation
3. 山区 shānqū (n.) mountainous area; mountains
4. 海边 hǎibiān (n.) seaside; beach
5. 爬 pá (v.) climb
6. 山 shān (n.) mountain; hill
7. 西部 xībù (n.) west
8. 凉快 liángkuai (adj.) cool

David, Wang Jiaming, Jack and Mary are talking about where to spend their summer vacation.

大卫：家明，你去哪儿度暑假？
dà wèi jiā míng nǐ qù nǎr dù shǔ jià

家明：我去山区度暑假。你去不去？
jiā míng wǒ qù shān qū dù shǔ jià nǐ qù bu qù

大卫：我不去，我去海边游泳。
dà wèi wǒ bú qù wǒ qù hǎi biān yóu yǒng

杰克：我喜欢爬山，我和你一起去山区。玛丽，你去哪儿？
jié kè wǒ xǐ huan pá shān wǒ hé nǐ yì qǐ qù shān qū mǎ lì nǐ qù nǎr

玛丽：我去西部海边，那里很凉快，还可以游泳。
mǎ lì wǒ qù xī bù hǎi biān nà li hěn liáng kuai hái kě yǐ yóu yǒng

Answer the following questions.

1. 王 家 明 打 算 去 度 暑 假 吗?
   wáng jiā míng dǎ suàn qù dù shǔ jià ma
2. 他 打 算 去 哪 儿 度 假?
   tā dǎ suàn qù nǎr dù jià
3. 杰 克 打 算 去 哪 儿 度 暑 假? 为 什 么?
   jié kè dǎ suàn qù nǎr dù shǔ jià wèi shén me
4. 玛 丽 打 算 去 哪 儿 度 暑 假? 为 什 么?
   mǎ lì dǎ suàn qù nǎr dù shǔ jià wèi shén me

Match the following places with the sports.

huáxuě

山 区
shān qū

海 边
hǎi biān

shātānpáiqiú

yóuyǒng

fānbǎn

páshān

An awful summer vacation

家 明:
jiā míng

你 好!
nǐ hǎo

你 在 山 区 度 暑 假 吗? 我 和 大 卫 在 西 部 海 边 度
nǐ zài shān qū dù shǔ jià ma wǒ hé dà wèi zài xī bù hǎi biān dù

暑 假。海 边 很 漂 亮,可 是 我 很 不 高 兴,因 为 最 近 经 常
shǔ jià hǎi biān hěn piào liang kě shì wǒ hěn bù gāo xìng yīn wèi zuì jìn jīng cháng

下 雨。山 区 怎 么 样? 凉 快 吗?
xià yǔ shān qū zěn me yàng liáng kuai ma

祝 你 暑 假 快 乐!
zhù nǐ shǔ jià kuài lè

你 的 好 朋 友: 玛 丽
nǐ de hǎo péng you mǎ lì

Class activity

Find out how your classmates usually spend their holidays and work out a plan of how you are going to spend your summer vacation.

Phonetics

1. Listen to the tape, and then answer the following questions.

(1) Where is Mary going to spend her summer vacation? Why?
(2) Where is Mrs. Lin going to spend her vacation? Why?
(3) Where is David going to spend his vacation? Why?

2. Read aloud the following limerick.

柜 里 有 个 盘 儿，
guì li yǒu ge pánr

盘 儿 里 有 个 碗 儿，
pánr li yǒu ge wǎnr

碗 儿 里 有 个 勺 儿，
wǎnr li yǒu ge sháor

勺 儿 里 有 个 豆 儿，
sháor li yǒu ge dòur

小 孩 儿 爱 吃 豆 儿。
xiǎo háir ài chī dòur

There's a plate in the cabinet,
a bowl in the plate,
a spoon in the bowl,
a bean in the spoon.
Kids like beans.

Learn to write

1. Structure of Chinese characters

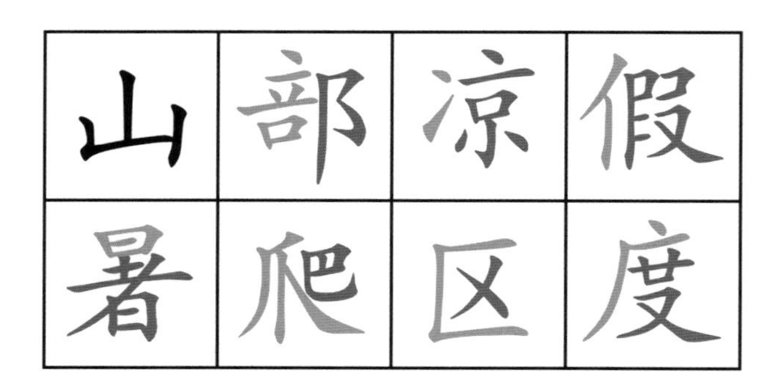

2. Examples of components

部件 bù jiàn	甲骨文 jiǎ gǔ wén	金文 jīn wén	小篆 xiǎo zhuàn	楷书 kǎi shū	组字 zǔ zì
者				者	暑
爪				爪	爬
京				京	凉

36 运动场上有很多人

yùn dòng chǎng shang yǒu hěn duō rén

Look and Say

New words

1. 学校	xuéxiào	(n.)	school
2. 举行	jǔxíng	(v.)	hold (a meeting, ceremony, etc.)
3. 运动会	yùndònghuì	(n.)	sports meet
4. 运动场	yùndòngchǎng	(n.)	sports ground; playground
5. 有的	yǒude	(pron.)	some
6. 参加	cānjiā	(v.)	take part in; participate in
7. 棒球	bàngqiú	(n.)	baseball
8. 赛	sài	(n.)	match; contest; competition
9. 网球	wǎngqiú	(n.)	tennis
10. 运动员	yùndòngyuán	(n.)	sportsman; sportswoman; athlete; player
11. 每次	měi cì		every time
12. 比赛	bǐsài	(n.)	match; contest; competition
13. 得	dé	(v.)	get; gain; win
14. 拉拉队	lālāduì	(n.)	cheering squad
15. 送	sòng	(v.)	send; deliver

An excerpt from Wang Jiaming's diary.

Diary

今天学校举行运动会。运动场上有很多人，有的参加棒球赛，有的参加网球赛。杰克是棒球运动员，每次比赛他都参加。大卫是网球运动员，他经常得第一。玛丽参加拉拉队，我给大家送饮料。我喜欢我们学校和我的同学。

Diary

Jīntiān xuéxiào jǔxíng yùndònghuì. Yùndòngchǎng shang yǒu hěn duō rén, yǒude cānjiā bàngqiú sài, yǒude cānjiā wǎngqiú sài. Jiékè shì bàngqiú yùndòngyuán, měicì bǐsài tā dōu cānjiā. Dàwèi shì wǎngqiú yùndòngyuán, tā jīngcháng dé dìyī. Mǎlì cānjiā lālāduì, wǒ gěi dàjiā sòng yǐnliào. Wǒ xǐhuan wǒmen xuéxiào hé wǒ de tóngxué.

Are there a lot of people here?

学校里有很多人
xué xiào lǐ yǒu hěn duō rén

比萨饼店
bǐ sà bǐng diàn

海边
hǎi biān

On your own: Make conversations according to the given words.

学校里有很多人，有的上课，有的参加运动会。
xué xiào lǐ yǒu hěn duō rén yǒu de shàng kè yǒu de cān jiā yùn dòng huì

1. 运动场上 yùn dòng chǎng shang
   参加比赛 cān jiā bǐ sài
   参加拉拉队 cān jiā lā lā duì
2. 海边 hǎi biān
   游泳 yóu yǒng
   休息 xiū xi

Give your own answers to the questions.

1. 你们学校经常举办体育比赛吗？
   nǐ men xué xiào jīng cháng jǔ bàn tǐ yù bǐ sài ma
2. 你喜欢什么体育比赛？
   nǐ xǐ huan shén me tǐ yù bǐ sài
3. 举办体育比赛的时候，你干什么？
   jǔ bàn tǐ yù bǐ sài de shí hou nǐ gàn shén me
4. 你们学校有拉拉队吗？有几个？他们参加什么比赛？
   nǐ men xué xiào yǒu lā lā duì ma yǒu jǐ ge tā men cān jiā shén me bǐ sài

Class activity: Chinese competition in the Forbidden City.

This will test how many Chinese characters you recognize after one year's study. See the appendix for further details on how to play this game.

Phonetics

1. Listen to the tape, and then answer the following questions.

(1) When is the school's sports meet going to be held?
(2) What match does the first boy take part in?
(3) What match does the second boy take part in?
(4) What match does Mary take part in?
(5) Does the boy, the last speaker, take part in any matches?

2. Read aloud the following children's song.

门 前 一 棵 葡 萄 树，
mén qián yì kē pú tao shù

嫩 嫩 绿 绿 刚 发 芽。
nèn nèn lǜ lǜ gāng fā yá

蜗 牛 背 着 重 重 的 壳，
wō niú bēi zhe zhòng zhòng de ké

一 步 一 步 往 上 爬。
yí bù yí bù wǎng shàng pá

树 上 两 只 黄 鹂 鸟，
shù shàng liǎng zhī huáng lí niǎo

嘻 嘻 哈 哈 在 笑 它，
xī xī hā hā zài xiào tā

葡 萄 成 熟 还 早 得 很，
pú tao chéng shú hái zǎo de hěn

现 在 上 来 干 什 么？
xiàn zài shàng lái gàn shén me

黄 鹂 黄 鹂 不 要 笑，
huáng lí huáng lí bù yào xiào

等 我 爬 上 它 就 成 熟 了。
děng wǒ pá shàng tā jiù chéng shú le

There is grape trellis in the yard. Sprouts have just come out, so green and tender. A snail is climbing up the trellis with her heavy shell in a great labor. Two orioles in the tree are laughing at her, "The grapes are far from being ripe. What're you climbing up for?" "Don't mock at me. They'll be ripe when I get there."

Can you sing it?

Learn to write

1. Structure of Chinese characters

场	棒	次	加	得
队	拉	员	举	参
赛	网	送		

2. Examples of components

部件 bù jiàn	甲骨文 jiǎ gǔ wén	金文 jīn wén	小篆 xiǎo zhuàn	楷书 kǎi shū	组字 zǔ zì
贝	[illegible]	[illegible]	[illegible]	贝(貝)	赛
奉	[illegible]	[illegible]	[illegible]	奉	棒

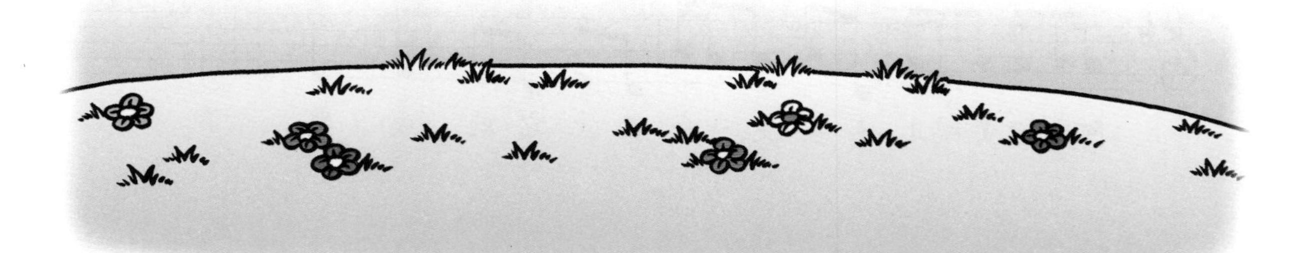

UNIT SUMMARY

FUNCTIONAL USAGE

1. Inquiring one's physical conditions

你 哪 儿 疼？
nǐ nǎr téng

我 左 腿 疼。
wǒ zuǒ tuǐ téng

2. Inquring about the exact location

上 面 还 是 下 面？
shàng mian hái shi xià mian

左 边 还 是 右 边？
zuǒ bian hái shi yòu bian

3. How to say ordinal number

右 边 第 三 颗。
yòu bian dì sān kē

4. Inquring about and offering one's favorite sports

你 喜 欢 什 么 运 动？
nǐ xǐ huan shén me yùn dòng

我 喜 欢 跑 步。
wǒ xǐ huan pǎo bù

5. Asking for directions

去 游 泳 池 怎 么 走？
qù yóu yǒng chí zěn me zǒu

6. Inquiring about and explaining one' holiday plan

你 去 哪 儿 度 暑 假？
nǐ qù nǎr dù shǔ jià

我 去 山 区 度 暑 假。
wǒ qù shān qū dù shǔ jià

7. Describing the process and scene of an activity

运 动 场 上 有 很 多 人，有 的 参 加 棒 球 赛，
yùn dòng chǎng shang yǒu hěn duō rén yǒu de cān jiā bàng qiú sài

有 的 参 加 网 球 赛。
yǒu de cān jiā wǎng qiú sài

GRAMMAR FOCUS

Sentence pattern	Example
1. 我左腿疼。 wǒ zuǒ tuǐ téng	
2. 有点儿…… yǒu diǎnr	我的头有点儿疼。 wǒ de tóu yǒu diǎnr téng
3. 会…… huì	你会游泳吗? nǐ huì yóu yǒng ma
4. 要是…… yào shi	要是有时间，你教我好吗? yào shi yǒu shí jiān nǐ jiāo wǒ hǎo ma
5. 在…… zài	我在那儿等你。 wǒ zài nàr děng nǐ
6. 去…… (v.) qù	我去海边游泳。 wǒ qù hǎi biān yóu yǒng
7. ……有…… yǒu	操场上有很多人。 cāo chǎngshang yǒu hěn duō rén

Appendix

I Class Activity

1. Flying Chess of Chinese

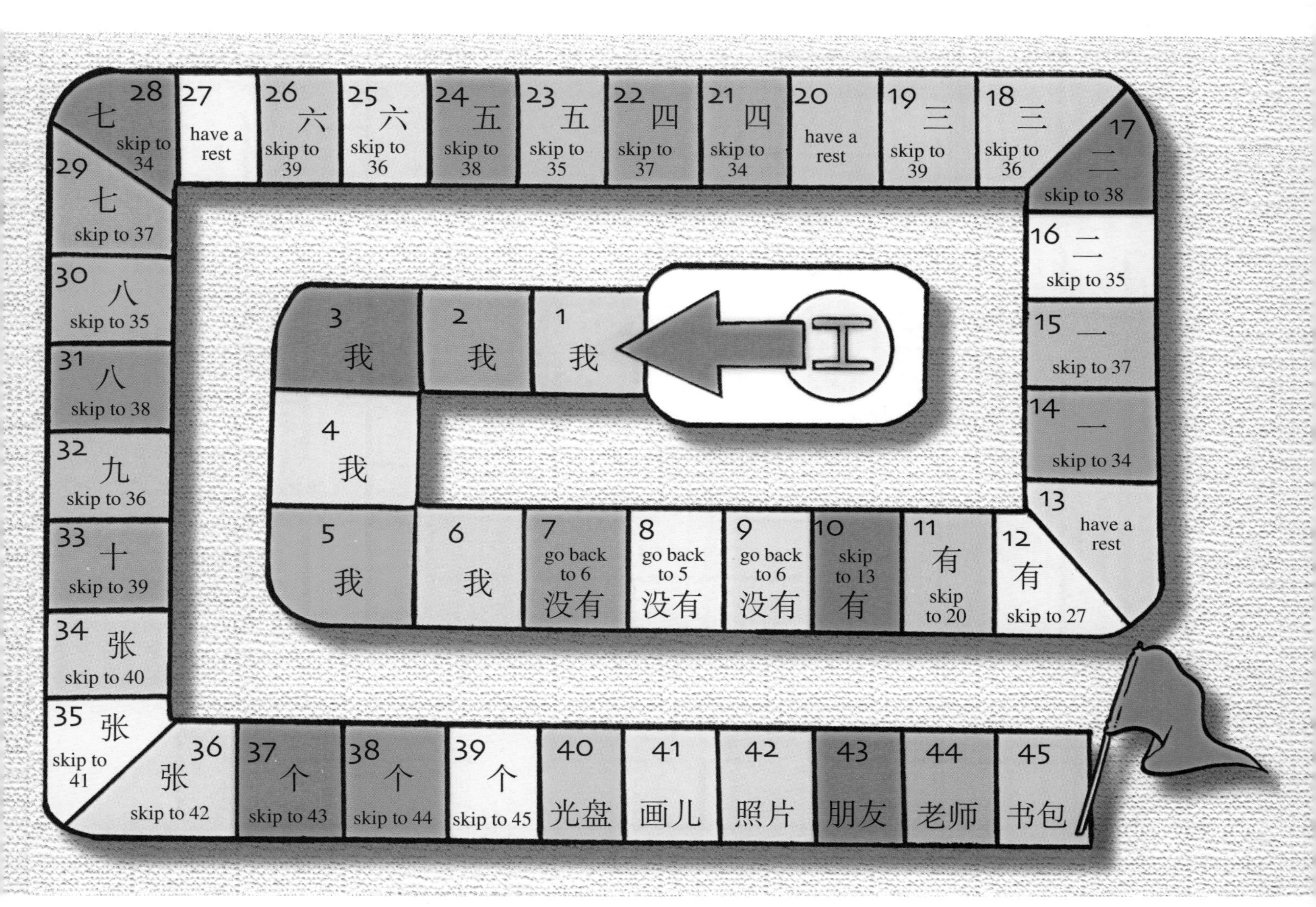

Divide the students into several groups, each of which contains 2-3 people. The students in the group will take turns to cast the dice, and then write down the sentence when they get a complete one. For example, "wǒ yǒu ________." The one who first "has" something and who "has" the most wins.

2. A Maze of Color

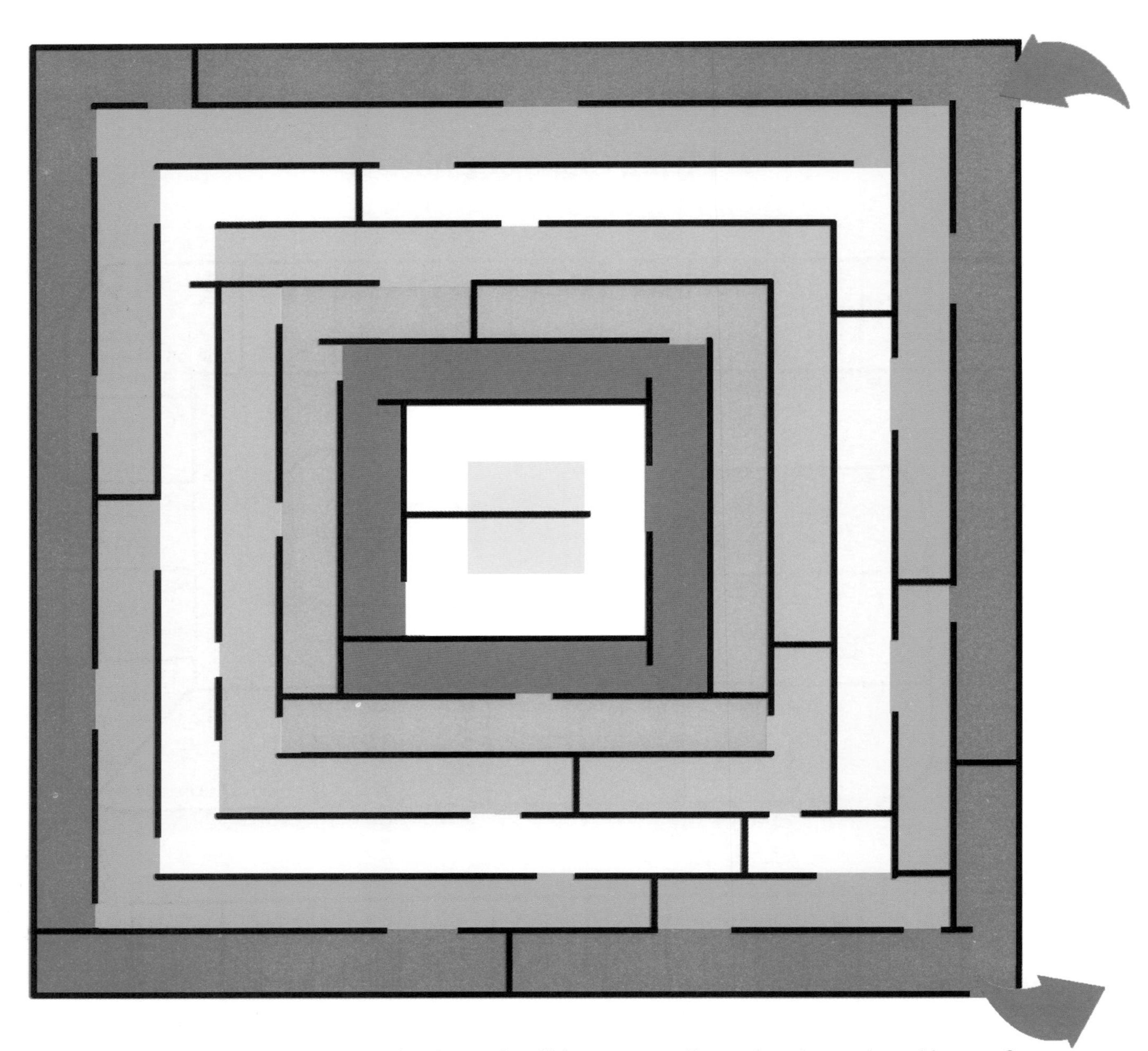

Please try this maze of color. ①Write down the Chinese name for each color and read it out after you have gone through the maze for the first time. ②Have a few more trials to see how many routes you can find.

3. Chinese Competition in the Forbidden City

Introductions

Now that over 300 Chinese words have been introduced after one year's study, we selected some of them and put them into the houses of the Forbidden City to see if you can recognize them and figure out their meanings.

The Forbidden City is located in the center of Beijing, and composed of 3 front halls, 3 back halls and an imperial garden. There are more than 9,000 houses in the City, which means an adult would turn out to be an old person after he/she stayed in each of these houses for only one night.

For the convenience of designing this game, we just drew an approximate layout of the 3 front halls of the City instead of the exact design of the whole. However, if you are interested in the Forbidden City, you may further read related materials or you may even pay a visit to Beijing to see it with your own eyes.

Instructions

First two people will cast dice. The one who has bigger number starts the game. The two people will enter the City from the two small gates respectively. During the whole game they will take turns to cast dice and find the corresponding house. The one who works out the pronunciation and meaning of the word in the house successfully will cast dice again; otherwise he / she will have to remain in the previous house and wait till the next turn. They will check each other's answers. The one who first reaches Hall I wins the game.

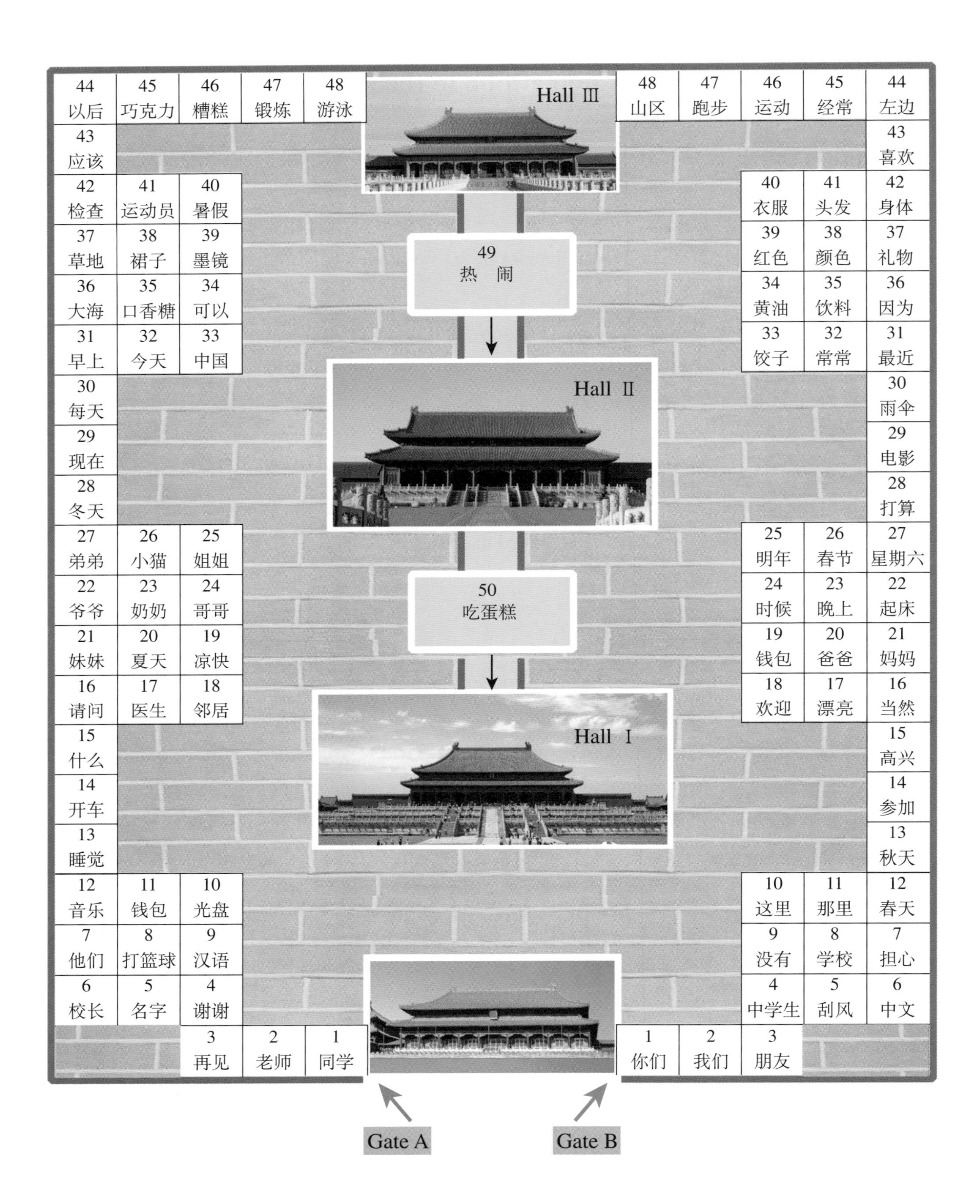
Hall Ⅲ
Hall Ⅱ
Hall Ⅰ
49 热　闹
50 吃蛋糕
44 以后
45 巧克力
46 糟糕
47 锻炼
48 游泳
43 应该
42 检查
41 运动员
40 暑假
37 草地
38 裙子
39 墨镜
36 大海
35 口香糖
34 可以
31 早上
32 今天
33 中国
30 每天
29 现在
28 冬天
27 弟弟
26 小猫
25 姐姐
22 爷爷
23 奶奶
24 哥哥
21 妹妹
20 夏天
19 凉快
16 请问
17 医生
18 邻居
15 什么
14 开车
13 睡觉
12 音乐
11 钱包
10 光盘
7 他们
8 打篮球
9 汉语
6 校长
5 名字
4 谢谢
3 再见
2 老师
1 同学
48 山区
47 跑步
46 运动
45 经常
44 左边
43 喜欢
40 衣服
41 头发
42 身体
39 红色
38 颜色
37 礼物
34 黄油
35 饮料
36 因为
33 饺子
32 常常
31 最近
30 雨伞
29 电影
28 打算
25 明年
26 春节
27 星期六
24 时候
23 晚上
22 起床
19 钱包
20 爸爸
21 妈妈
18 欢迎
17 漂亮
16 当然
15 高兴
14 参加
13 秋天
10 这里
11 那里
12 春天
9 没有
8 学校
7 担心
4 中学生
5 刮风
6 中文
1 你们
2 我们
3 朋友
Gate A
Gate B

The Keys to A's Questions

1.tóngxué classmate
2. lǎoshī teacher
3. zàijiàn good-bye
4. xièxie thank
5. míngzi name
6. xiàozhǎng principal
7. tāmen they, them
8. dǎ lánqiú play basketball
9. Hànyǔ Chinese
10. guāngpán disks
11. qiánbāo wallet
12. yīnyuè music
13. shuì jiào sleep
14. kāi chē drive
15. shénme what
16. qǐng wèn May I ask?
17. yīshēng doctor
18. línjū neighbor
19. liángkuai cool
20. xiàtiān summer
21. mèimei younger sister
22. yéye grandfather
23. nǎinai grandmother
24. gēge elder brother
25. jiějie elder sister
26. xiǎo māo little cat
27. dìdi younger brother
28. dōngtiān winter
29. xiànzài now
30. měi tiān every day
31. zǎoshang morning
32. jīntiān today
33. Zhōngguó China
34. kěyǐ may
35. kǒuxiāngtáng chewing gum
36. dàhǎi sea
37. cǎodì grassland
38. qúnzi dress
39. mòjìng sunglasses
40. shǔjià summer vacation
41. yùndòngyuán athlete
42. jiǎnchá check
43. yīnggāi should
44. yǐhòu after
45. qiǎokèlì chocolate
46. zāogāo too bad
47. duànliàn do exercises
48. yóuyǒng swim
49. rènao bustling
50. chī dàngāo eat cake

The Keys to B's Questions

1. nǐmen you
2. wǒmen we, us
3. péngyou friend
4. zhōngxuéshēng high school student
5. guā fēng (of wind) blow
6. Zhōngwén Chinese
7. dānxīn worry
8. xuéxiào school
9. méiyǒu not to have
10. zhèlǐ here
11. nàli there
12. chūntiān spring
13. qiūtiān autumn
14. cānjiā take part in
15. gāoxìng happy
16. dāngrán of course
17. piàoliang beautiful
18. huānyíng welcome
19. qiánbāo wallet
20. bàba father
21. māma mother
22. qǐchuáng get up
23. wǎnshang night
24. shíhou time
25. míngnián next year
26. Chūn Jié the Spring Festival
27. xīngqīliù saturday
28. dǎsuàn plan
29. diànyǐng film
30. yǔsǎn umbrella
31. zuìjìn recently
32. chángcháng often
33. jiǎozi dumpling
34. huángyóu butter
35. yǐnliào drinks
36. yīnwèi because
37. lǐwù gift
38. yánsè color
39. hóngsè red
40. yīfu clothes
41. tóufa hair
42. shēntǐ body
43. xǐhuan like
44. zuǒbian left
45. jīngcháng often
46. yùndòng sports
47. pǎobù jogging
48. shānqū mountains
49. rènao bustling
50. chī dàngāo eat cake

II Vocabulary

Word	*Pinyin*	Part of Speech	Translation	Lesson
啊	a	pt.	particle word	8
艾米丽	Àimǐlì	n.	Emily	8
吧	ba	pt.	particle word	19
爸爸	bàba	n.	dad;father	17
白色	báisè	n.	white	30
柏树街	Bǎishù jiē	n.	Cypress Street	16
半	bàn	num.	half	19
棒球	bàngqiú	n.	baseball	36
包	bāo	m.	measure word	27
北京	Běijīng	n.	Beijing	24
比萨饼	bǐsàbǐng	n.	pizza	16
比赛	bǐsài	n.	match; contest; competition	36
别	bié	adv.	don't	34
别的	biéde	pron.	else; other; another	27
不错	búcuò	adj.	not bad	29
不客气	bú kèqi		You're welcome.	4
参加	cānjiā	v.	take part in; participate in	36
草地	cǎodì	n.	grassland	28
长	cháng	adj.	long	30
常常	chángcháng	adv.	often	24
车牌	chēpái	n.	licence plate	30
橙色	chéngsè	n.	orange	28
吃	chī	v.	eat; have	12
穿	chuān	v.	wear	29
春节	Chūn Jié	n.	The Spring Festival (Chinese Lunar New Year)	21
春天	chūntiān	n.	spring	24
从	cóng	prep.	from	15

打	dǎ	v.	play	7
打算	dǎsuàn	n.;v.	plan (to); be going to	22
大	dà	adj.	big	17
大海	dàhǎi	n.	sea; ocean	28
大黄	Dàhuáng	n.	Big Yellow (usually a name for a dog or a cat)	14
大家	dàjiā	pron.	all, everybody	12
大卫	Dàwèi	n.	David	1
带	dài	v.	take/bring/carry...with sb.	23
戴	dài	v.	(of glasses, hats) wear	30
担心	dānxīn	v.	worry	34
蛋糕	dàngāo	n.	cake	12
当然	dāngrán	adv.	certainly; of course	13
到	dào	v.	arrive	16
得	dé	v.	get; gain; win	36
的	de	pt.	particle word	6
等	děng	v.	wait (for)	34
弟弟	dìdi	n.	younger brother	18
第	dì	af.	prefix	32
(一)点(儿)	(yì) diǎn(r)	m.	a little; a bit; some (here something)	25
点(钟)	diǎn (zhōng)	n.	o'clock	19
(商)店	(shāng) diàn	n.	(business)store; shop	16
电影	diànyǐng	n.	movie	22
东	dōng	n.	east	34
东西	dōngxi	n.	thing; stuff	26
冬天	dōngtiān	n.	winter	24
都	dōu	adv.	both; all	8
度	dù	v.	spend (holidays)	35

锻炼	duànliàn	v.	do exercises	33
对	duì	adj.	yes; that's right	10
多	duō	adj.	many; much	26
多大	duō dà		how old	13
多少	duōshao	pron.	how much; how many	10
法语	Fǎyǔ	n.	the French language	8
非常	fēicháng	adv.	very	24
份	fèn	m.	a set of	16
风	fēng	n.	wind	23
副	fù	m.	pair; set	30
感恩节	Gǎn' ēn Jié	n.	Thanksgiving Day	21
橄榄球	gǎnlǎnqiú	n.	American football	7
干	gàn	v.	do	22
高兴	gāoxìng	adj.	happy; glad; cheerful	12
哥哥	gēge	n.	elder brother	17
个	gè	m.	measure word	25
给	gěi	v.	give	10
跟	gēn	prep.	with	12
狗	gǒu	n.	dog	14
刮(风)	guā (fēng)	v.	(of wind)blow	23
拐	guǎi	v.	turn; change direction	34
光盘	guāngpán	n.	disks; CDs	9
果酱	guǒjiàng	n.	jam	27
过年	guònián	v.	celebrate the New Year or the Spring Festival	26
还	hái	adv.	and; as well; also; too	17
还是	háishi	conj.	or	29
海边	hǎibiān	n.	seaside; beach	35
汉语	Hànyǔ	n.	the Chinese language	8

好	hǎo	adj.	good	1
好	hǎo	adj.	ok; all right	16
号	hào	n.	number in a series	16
号	hào	n.	date	21
号码	hàomǎ	n.	number	30
喝	hē	v.	drink	25
和	hé	conj.	and	11
盒	hé	m.	box	27
黑色	hēisè	n.	black	29
很	hěn	adv.	very	12
红色	hóngsè	n.	red	28
后天	hòutiān	n.	the day after tomorrow	26
欢迎	huānyíng	v.	welcome	15
黄色	huángsè	n.	yellow	30
黄油	huángyóu	n.	butter	27
会	huì	v.;aux.	can	33
鸡蛋	jīdàn	n.	egg	25
几	jǐ	pron.	how many	9
家	jiā	n.	home	15
检查	jiǎnchá	v.	examine; check	31
件	jiàn	m.	piece	29
教	jiāo	v.	teach	33
饺子	jiǎozi	n.	dumpling	25
叫	jiào	v.	call; name	1
教练	jiàoliàn	n.	coach; instructor	7
节	jié	n.	holiday; festival	21
节日	jiérì	n.	holiday; red-letter day	24
杰克	Jiékè	n.	Jack	3
姐姐	jiějie	n.	elder sister	17

今天	jīntiān	n.	today	12
经常	jīngcháng	adv.	often	33
举行	jǔxíng	v.	hold (a meeting, ceremony, etc.)	36
觉得	juéde	v.	think; feel	24
开车	kāichē	v.	drive	13
看	kàn	v.	see; look at; watch	22
颗	kē	m.	measure word	32
可能	kěnéng	aux.	maybe; perhaps	23
可是	kěshì	conj.	but; however	18
可以	kěyǐ	aux.	can; may	22
刻(钟)	kè (zhōng)	n.	a quarter of an hour	20
口	kǒu	m.	measure word	17
口香糖	kǒuxiāngtáng	n.	chewing gum	27
块	kuài	m.	lump; piece	27
快乐	kuàilè	adj.	happy; joyous	11
拉拉队	lālāduì	n.	cheering squad	36
来	lái	v.	come	15
蓝色	lánsè	n.	blue	28
篮球	lánqiú	n.	basketball	7
老师	lǎoshī	n.	teacher	2
冷	lěng	adj.	cold	24
礼物	lǐwù	n.	present; gift	26
里	lǐ	n.	in; inside	10
凉快	liángkuai	adj.	cool	35
两	liǎng	num.	two	14
辆	liàng	m.	measure word	30
邻居	línjū	n.	neighbor	18
林(老师)	Lín (lǎoshī)	n.	a surname	2
路口	lùkǒu	n.	crossing; junction; intersection	34

绿色	lǜsè	n.	green	28
妈妈	māma	n.	mom; mother	17
马上	mǎshàng	adv.	right away	16
玛丽	Mǎlì	n.	Mary	3
吗	ma	pt.	particle word	5
买	mǎi	v.	buy	26
忙	máng	adj.	busy	24
猫	māo	n.	cat	17
没有	méiyǒu	v.	not to have; don't have	9
每次	měi cì		every time	36
每天	měi tiān		every day	20
妹妹	mèimei	n.	younger sister	18
们	men	suf.	suffix	2
面包	miànbāo	n.	bread	27
名字	míngzi	n.	name	4
明亮	míngliàng	adj.	bright	28
明年	míngnián	n.	next year	21
明天	míngtiān	n.	tomorrow	21
墨镜	mòjìng	n.	dark glasses; sunglasses	30
哪	nǎ	pron.	which	21
哪儿	nǎr	pron.	where	23
哪里	nǎli	pron.	where	11
那	nà	pron.	that	10
奶奶	nǎinai	n.	(paternal)grandmother	18
男	nán	adj.	man	30
呢	ne	pt.	particle word	15
你	nǐ	pron.	you	1
你们	nǐmen	pron.	you (plural)	3
年货	niánhuò	n.	special purchases for the	

			Spring Festival	26
您	nín	pron.	polite form of "you" (singular)	11
牛奶	niúnǎi	n.	milk	27
爬	pá	v.	climb	35
跑步	pǎobù	v.	jogging	33
配	pèi	v.	match; go well with	29
朋友	péngyou	n.	friend	6
漂亮	piàoliang	adj.	pretty	14
瓶	píng	m.	bottle	27
起床	qǐchuáng	v.	get up	19
钱	qián	n.	money	10
钱包	qiánbāo	n.	wallet; purse	10
巧克力	qiǎokèlì	n.	chocolate	32
请问	qǐngwèn	v.	May I ask?	16
秋天	qiūtiān	n.	fall	24
去	qù	v.	go	19
去年	qùnián	n.	last year	26
裙子	qúnzi	n.	dress	29
热	rè	adj.	hot	24
热闹	rènao	adj.	busy; bustling	26
人	rén	n.	person; people	17
日本	Rìběn	n.	Japan	15
如果	rúguǒ	conj.	if	29
赛	sài	n.	match; contest; competition	36
山	shān	n.	mountain; hill	35
山区	shānqū	n.	mountainous area; mountains	35
上面	shàngmian	n.	upper part	32
少	shǎo	adv.	few; little	32
身体	shēntǐ	n.	health;body	31

生日	shēngri	n.	birthday	11
什么	shénme	pron.	what	4
时候	shíhou	n.	time; moment	20
时间	shíjiān	n.	time	33
事	shì	n.	matter; affair; thing; business	19
是	shì	v.	be (is /am/ are)	3
收到	shōu dào		receive; get	26
舒服	shūfu	adj.	be well; comfortable	31
暑假	shǔjià	n.	summer vacation	35
树木	shùmù	n.	tree	28
谁	shuí	pron.	who	7
睡觉	shuìjiào	v.	go to bed; sleep	20
送	sòng	v.	send; deliver	36
岁	suì	m.	year (of age)	13
他	tā	pron.	he	3
它	tā	pron.	it	14
她	tā	pron.	she	3
他们	tāmen	pron.	they; them (male)	6
她们	tāmen	pron.	they; them (female)	5
汤	tāng	n.	soup	25
糖	táng	n.	candy	32
特别	tèbié	adv.	specially	32
疼	téng	v.	ache; hurt	31
天	tiān	n.	day	21
天气	tiānqì	n.	weather	23
听	tīng	v.	listen (to)	12
同学	tóngxué	n.	classmate	2
头	tóu	n.	head	31
头发	tóufa	n.	hair	30

腿	tuǐ	n.	leg	31
外面	wàimian	n.	outside	23
玩	wán	v.	play	15
晚上	wǎnshang	n.	night; evening	20
碗	wǎn	m.	bowl	25
王家明	Wáng Jiāmíng	n.	Wang Jiaming	1
网球	wǎngqiú	n.	tennis	36
为什么	wèishénme		why	26
喂	wèi	exd.	hello	16
温哥华	Wēngēhuá	n.	Vancouver	18
问题	wèntí	n.	problem	31
我	wǒ	pron.	I; me	1
我们	wǒmen	pron.	we; us	6
西部	xībù	n.	west	35
喜欢	xǐhuan	v.	like	18
下面	xiàmian	n.	lower part	32
下午	xiàwǔ	n.	afternoon	23
下雨	xià yǔ		rain	23
夏天	xiàtiān	n.	summer	24
先生	xiānsheng	n.	mister; sir; gentleman	25
现在	xiànzài	n.	now	19
向	xiàng	prep.	to; towards	34
小	xiǎo	adj.	small; little	17
小雨	Xiǎoyǔ	n.	a person's name, literally "drizzle"	24
校长	xiàozhǎng	n.	headmaster; principal; (university or college) president	5
谢谢	xièxie	v.	thank	4
新年	xīnnián	n.	New Year	24

星期	xīngqī	n.	day of the week	22
行	xíng	v.	will do; be all right	22
姓	xìng	v.	to be surnamed; surname	15
休息	xiūxi	v.	rest	31
学	xué	v.	learn; study	8
学生	xuésheng	n.	student	5
学校	xuéxiào	n.	school	36
压岁钱	yāsuìqián	n.	money given to children as a lunar New Year gift	26
牙	yá	n.	tooth	32
颜色	yánsè	n.	color	28
样子	yàngzi	n.	appearance; look	30
药	yào	n.	medicine	31
要	yào	v.	want; would like (to)	16
要是	yàoshi	conj.	if	33
爷爷	yéye	n.	(paternal) grandfather	18
也	yě	adv.	also; too	7
一共	yígòng	adv.	altogether	27
一起	yìqǐ	n.	together	12
一下儿	yíxiàr		once	31
衣服	yīfu	n.	clothes	29
医生	yīshēng	n.	doctor	18
以后	yǐhòu	n.	afterwards; after; later	32
因为	yīnwèi	conj.	because	26
音乐	yīnyuè	n.	music	12
饮料	yǐnliào	n.	beverage	25
应该	yīnggāi	v.;aux.	should	32
用	yòng	v.	use	26
游泳	yóuyǒng	v.	swim	33

游泳池	yóuyǒngchí	n.	swimming pool	34
有	yǒu	v.	have	8
有的	yǒude	pron.	some	36
有点儿	yǒudiǎnr	adv.	a bit; rather	31
右	yòu	n.	right	34
右边	yòubian	n.	right	32
雨伞	yǔsǎn	n.	umbrella	23
雨衣	yǔyī	n.	raincoat	23
元	yuán	m.	measure word	10
月	yuè	n.	month	21
运动	yùndòng	n.	sports	33
运动场	yùndòngchǎng	n.	sports ground; playground	36
运动会	yùndònghuì	n.	sports meet	36
运动员	yùndòngyuán	n.	sportsman; sportswoman; athlete; player	36
在	zài	v.	be	11
在	zài	prep.	(indicating where a person or thing is)	16
再见	zàijiàn	v.	see you; good-bye	2
糟糕	zāogāo	adj.	terrible; too bad	32
早上	zǎoshang	n.	morning	20
怎么	zěnme	pron.	how	34
怎么样	zěnmeyàng	pron.	how	23
张	zhāng	m.	measure word	9
找	zhǎo	v.	to find; to look for	11
找	zhǎo	v.	give change	27
这	zhè	pron.	this	10
这里	zhèlǐ	pron.	here	11
芝加哥	Zhījiāgē	n.	Chicago	18
中国	Zhōngguó	n.	China	21

中文	Zhōngwén	n.	Chinese	9
中学生	zhōngxuéshēng	n.	high school student	6
种	zhǒng	m.	kind; sort; type	28
住	zhù	v.	live; reside	16
祝	zhù	v.	offer good wishes; wish	11
紫色	zǐsè	n.	purple	30
走	zǒu	v.	walk; get (to)	34
最	zuì	adv.	most; least; best; to the highest or lowest degree	24
最近	zuìjìn	n.	recently; lately	24
昨天	zuótiān	n.	yesterday	21
左	zuǒ	n.	left	31

（共320个）

III Chinese Characters

Characters		Pinyin	Lesson	Characters		Pinyin	Lesson
啊	啊	a	8	打	打	dǎ	7
吧	吧	ba	19	大	大	dà	1
爸	爸	bà	17	带	帶	dài	23
白	白	bái	30	戴	戴	dài	30
半	半	bàn	19	担	擔	dān	34
棒	棒	bàng	36	蛋	蛋	dàn	12
包	包	bāo	10	当	當	dāng	13
边	邊	biān	32	得	得	dé	36
别	别	bié	27	等	等	děng	34
不	不	bù	4	地	地	dì	28
步	步	bù	33	弟	弟	dì	18
部	部	bù	35	第	第	dì	32
参	參	cān	36	点	點	diǎn	19
草	草	cǎo	28	电	電	diàn	22
查	查	chá	31	店	店	diàn	16
长	長	cháng	30	东	東	dōng	26
常	常	cháng	24	冬	冬	dōng	24
场	場	chǎng	36	动	動	dòng	33
车	車	chē	13	都	都	dōu	8
橙	橙	chéng	28	度	度	dù	35
吃	吃	chī	12	锻	鍛	duàn	33
池	池	chí	34	队	隊	duì	36
穿	穿	chuān	29	对	對	duì	10
床	床	chuáng	19	多	多	duō	10
春	春	chūn	21	恩	恩	ēn	21
次	次	cì	36	法	法	fǎ	8
从	從	cóng	15	发	髮	fà	30
错	錯	cuò	29	非	非	fēi	24

份	份	fèn	16
服	服	fú	29
副	副	fù	30
该	該	gāi	32
感	感	gǎn	21
橄	橄	gǎn	7
干	幹	gàn	22
高	高	gāo	12
糕	糕	gāo	12
哥	哥	gē	17
个	個	gè	25
给	給	gěi	10
跟	跟	gēn	22
共	共	gòng	27
狗	狗	gǒu	14
刮	颳	guā	23
拐	拐	guǎi	34
光	光	guāng	9
国	國	guó	21
果	果	guǒ	27
过	過	guò	26
还	還	hái	17
海	海	hǎi	28
汉	漢	hàn	8
好	好	hǎo	1
号	號	hào	16
喝	喝	hē	25
和	和	hé	11
盒	盒	hé	27
黑	黑	hēi	29
很	很	hěn	12
红	紅	hóng	28
后	後	hòu	26
候	候	hòu	20
欢	歡	huān	15
黄	黃	huáng	14
会	會	huì	33
鸡	雞	jī	25
几	幾	jǐ	9
加	加	jiā	36
家	家	jiā	1
假	假	jià	35
检	檢	jiǎn	31
见	見	jiàn	2
件	件	jiàn	29
酱	醬	jiàng	27
教	教	jiāo	33
饺	餃	jiǎo	25
叫	叫	jiào	1
觉	覺	jiào	20
节	節	jié	21
杰	傑	jié	3
姐	姐	jiě	17
今	今	jīn	12
经	經	jīng	33
镜	鏡	jìng	30
居	居	jū	18
举	舉	jǔ	36

觉	覺	jué	24	料	料	liào	25
开	開	kāi	30	邻	鄰	lín	18
看	看	kàn	22	林	林	lín	2
颗	顆	kē	32	路	路	lù	34
可	可	kě	18	绿	綠	lǜ	28
克	剋	kè	3	妈	媽	mā	17
客	客	kè	4	玛	瑪	mǎ	3
刻	刻	kè	20	码	碼	mǎ	30
口	口	kǒu	17	吗	嗎	ma	5
块	塊	kuài	27	买	買	mǎi	26
快	快	kuài	11	忙	忙	máng	24
拉	拉	lā	36	猫	貓	māo	17
来	來	lái	15	么	麼	me	4
蓝	藍	lán	28	没	沒	méi	9
篮	籃	lán	7	每	每	měi	20
榄	欖	lǎn	7	妹	妹	mèi	18
老	老	lǎo	2	们	們	men	2
乐	樂	lè	11	面	面	miàn	23
冷	冷	lěng	24	名	名	míng	4
礼	禮	lǐ	26	明	明	míng	1
里	裏	lǐ	10	墨	墨	mò	30
力	力	lì	32	木	木	mù	28
丽	麗	lì	3	哪	哪	nǎ	11
炼	煉	liàn	33	那	那	nà	10
练	練	liàn	34	奶	奶	nǎi	18
凉	涼	liáng	35	男	男	nán	30
两	兩	liǎng	14	闹	鬧	nào	26
亮	亮	liàng	14	呢	呢	ne	15
辆	輛	liàng	30	能	能	néng	23

你	你	nǐ	1	色	色	sè	28
年	年	nián	21	山	山	shān	35
您	您	nín	11	上	上	shàng	20
牛	牛	niú	27	少	少	shǎo	10
爬	爬	pá	35	身	身	shēn	31
牌	牌	pái	30	生	生	shēng	5
盘	盤	pán	9	师	師	shī	2
跑	跑	pǎo	33	什	什	shén	4
配	配	pèi	29	时	時	shí	20
朋	朋	péng	6	事	事	shì	19
漂	漂	piào	14	是	是	shì	3
瓶	瓶	píng	27	收	收	shōu	26
期	期	qī	22	舒	舒	shū	31
起	起	qǐ	12	暑	暑	shǔ	35
气	氣	qì	4	树	樹	shù	28
钱	錢	qián	10	谁	誰	shuí	7
巧	巧	qiǎo	32	睡	睡	shuì	20
秋	秋	qiū	24	送	送	sòng	36
球	球	qiú	7	算	算	suàn	22
区	區	qū	35	岁	歲	suì	13
去	去	qù	19	他	他	tā	5
裙	裙	qún	29	她	她	tā	5
然	然	rán	13	它	它	tā	14
热	熱	rè	24	汤	湯	tāng	25
人	人	rén	17	糖	糖	táng	27
日	日	rì	12	特	特	tè	32
如	如	rú	29	疼	疼	téng	31
赛	賽	sài	36	题	題	tí	31
伞	傘	sǎn	23	体	體	tǐ	31

天	天	tiān	12
听	聽	tīng	12
同	同	tóng	2
头	頭	tóu	30
腿	腿	tuǐ	31
外	外	wài	23
玩	玩	wán	15
碗	碗	wǎn	25
王	王	wáng	1
网	網	wǎng	36
为	為	wèi	26
卫	衛	wèi	1
喂	喂	wèi	16
文	文	wén	9
我	我	wǒ	1
午	午	wǔ	23
物	物	wù	26
西	西	xī	26
息	息	xī	31
喜	喜	xǐ	18
下	下	xià	23
夏	夏	xià	24
先	先	xiān	25
现	現	xiàn	19
香	香	xiāng	27
向	向	xiàng	34
小	小	xiǎo	17
校	校	xiào	5
谢	謝	xiè	4
心	心	xīn	34
新	新	xīn	24
行	行	xíng	22
兴	興	xìng	12
姓	姓	xìng	15
休	休	xiū	31
学	學	xué	2
牙	牙	yá	32
颜	顏	yán	28
样	樣	yàng	23
药	藥	yào	31
要	要	yào	16
爷	爺	yé	18
也	也	yě	7
一	一	yī	12
衣	衣	yī	29
医	醫	yī	18
以	以	yǐ	22
因	因	yīn	26
音	音	yīn	12
饮	飲	yǐn	25
应	應	yīng	32
迎	迎	yíng	15
影	影	yǐng	22
泳	泳	yǒng	33
用	用	yòng	26
油	油	yóu	27
游	游	yóu	33
友	友	yǒu	6

有	有	yǒu	8	长	長	zhǎng	5
雨	雨	yǔ	23	找	找	zhǎo	11
语	語	yǔ	8	这	這	zhè	10
元	元	yuán	10	中	中	zhōng	6
员	員	yuán	36	住	住	zhù	16
月	月	yuè	21	祝	祝	zhù	11
乐	樂	yuè	12	子	子	zǐ	25
再	再	zài	2	紫	紫	zǐ	30
在	在	zài	11	字	字	zì	4
糟	糟	zāo	32	走	走	zǒu	34
早	早	zǎo	20	最	最	zuì	24
怎	怎	zěn	34	昨	昨	zuó	21
张	張	zhāng	9				

（共 313 个）

Table of Combinations of Initials and Finals in *Putonghua*

Initial \ Final	-i(ɿ、ʅ)	a	o	e	er	ai	ei	ao	ou	an	en	ang	eng	ong
b		ba	bo			bai	bei	bao		ban	ben	bang	beng	
p		pa	po			pai	pei	pao	pou	pan	pen	pang	peng	
m		ma	mo	me		mai	mei	mao	mou	man	men	mang	meng	
f		fa	fo				fei		fou	fan	fen	fang	feng	
d		da		de		dai	dei	dao	dou	dan		dang	deng	dong
t		ta		te		tai		tao	tou	tan		tang	teng	tong
n		na		ne		nai	nei	nao	nou	nan	nen	nang	neng	nong
l		la		le		lai	lei	lao	lou	lan		lang	leng	long
g		ga		ge		gai	gei	gao	gou	gan	gen	gang	geng	gong
k		ka		ke		kai	kei	kao	kou	kan	ken	kang	keng	kong
h		ha		he		hai	hei	hao	hou	han	hen	hang	heng	hong
j														
q														
x														
zh	zhi	zha		zhe		zhai	zhei	zhao	zhou	zhan	zhen	zhang	zheng	zhong
ch	chi	cha		che		chai		chao	chou	chan	chen	chang	cheng	chong
sh	shi	sha		she		shai	shei	shao	shou	shan	shen	shang	sheng	
r	ri			re				rao	rou	ran	ren	rang	reng	rong
z	zi	za		ze		zai		zao	zou	zan	zen	zang	zeng	zong
c	ci	ca		ce		cai		cao	cou	can	cen	cang	ceng	cong
s	si	sa		se		sai		sao	sou	san	sen	sang	seng	song
		a	o	e	er	ai	ei	ao	ou	an	en	ang	eng	

Initial \ Final	i	ia	ie	iao	iou	ian	in	iang	ing	iong
b	bi		bie	biao		bian	bin		bing	
p	pi		pie	piao		pian	pin		ping	
m	mi		mie	miao	miu	mian	min		ming	
f										
d	di		die	diao	diu	dian			ding	
t	ti		tie	tiao		tian			ting	
n	ni		nie	niao	niu	nian	nin	niang	ning	
l	li	lia	lie	liao	liu	lian	lin	liang	ling	
g										
k										
h										
j	ji	jia	jie	jiao	jiu	jian	jin	jiang	jing	jiong
q	qi	qia	qie	qiao	qiu	qian	qin	qiang	qing	qiong
x	xi	xia	xie	xiao	xiu	xian	xin	xiang	xing	xiong
zh										
ch										
sh										
r										
z										
c										
s										
	yi	ya	ye	yao	you	yan	yin	yang	ying	yong

Initial \ Final	u	ua	uo	uai	uei	uan	uen	uang	ueng	ü	üe	uan	ün
b	bu												
p	pu												
m	mu												
f	fu												
d	du		duo		dui	duan	dun						
t	tu		tuo		tui	tuan	tun						
n	nu		nuo			nuan				nü	nüe		
l	lu		luo			luan	lun			lü	lüe		
g	gu	gua	guo	guai	gui	guan	gun	guang					
k	ku	kua	kuo	kuai	kui	kuan	kun	kuang					
h	hu	hua	huo	huai	hui	huan	hun	huang					
j										ju	jue	juan	jun
q										qu	que	quan	qun
x										xu	xue	xuan	xun
zh	zhu	zhua	zhuo	zhuai	zhui	zhuan	zhun	zhuang					
ch	chu	chua	chuo	chuai	chui	chuan	chun	chuang					
sh	shu	shua	shuo	shuai	shui	shuan	shun	shuang					
r	ru	rua	ruo		rui	ruan	run						
z	zu		zuo		zui	zuan	zun						
c	cu		cuo		cui	cuan	cun						
s	su		suo		sui	suan	sun						
	wu	wa	wo	wai	wei	wan	wen	wang	weng	yu	yue	yuan	yun